Random Thoughts

Engage · Learn · Grow · Achieve

Robin Anne Griffiths

Random Thoughts

Engage · Learn · Grow · Achieve

Robin Anne Griffiths

ISBN-13: 978-0692129456

Dedication

Have you ever thought about the teachers and mentors in your life? I have had many who guided me. I believe each of them were brought into my life for a reason. It was either to provide a lesson or give guidance. Some of these lessons were learned when given and others discovered later when needed. I am thankful and appreciative of the teachings given whether intentionally or not by all the people who have touched my life.

This book is dedicated to all those who are helping others with life's lessons. The greatest gift is given from someone who helps you understand and grow as an individual.

CONTENTS

Introduction.. 1

Changing... 7

Past, Present And Future........................... 9

The Little Things In Life............................ 11

The Messages You Are Sending................. 13

Listen To Your Gut................................... 17

Mountain Of Lessons................................ 19

Small Changes Can Bring Big Change......... 23

What Others Can Teach Us........................ 27

Saying I Did It... 31

Getting What You Want............................. 35

Leading And Inspiring............................... 39

Thriving Not Just Surviving........................ 41

In and Out Of Balance............................... 45

How's That Working Out?.......................... 49

Changing Your Attitude............................. 51

Find The Perfect Fit.................................. 53

Positive Problems.................................... 55

What Did You Say?................................... 57

First Impressions Are Lasting Impressions........... 61

Aggravation!... 63

Find Your Passion.................................... 65

Play Well With Others............................... 69

Find Your Motivation.. 71

Good As Your Word.. 73

Mind Your own Business................................... 75

I Wish... 79

Making A Game Plan... 81

The Air Around You.. 85

Cleaning Out The Cobwebs................................ 87

Magic Words.. 89

Get It Done... 91

Tomorrow Is Another Day.................................. 95

Finding Your Path.. 97

Where Are You Going?....................................... 99

It's Not A Secret.. 101

Make A Plan.. 103

What's In It For Me?... 105

The Magic Pill.. 107

Making Each Day A Gift..................................... 109

Silver Linings.. 111

Day To Day... 115

Dump The Clutter.. 119

The Judge... 121

Salty Nose.. 123

The Power Of Words... 125

Making Connections 127

Take The Step... 131

It's A Dog's World.................................... 133

Patience...Please.................................... 137

Cherished Moments................................ 139

Did You Say No?..................................... 141

What Goes Around 145

Discovering The World............................ 149

Doing Things Differently......................... 151

Having Gratitude.................................... 155

Begin Anew.. 159

Racing To Nowhere................................ 163

Life Goes On... 167

Role Models... 169

Overwhelmed? The Overcome.............. 173

Getting Back From Giving....................... 177

Giving and Getting................................. 179

Managing Transition.............................. 181

Setting Your Compass............................ 185

Find Your Road Map 187

Checks And Balances.............................. 189

Finding The Joy In Your Life.................... 193

Dare To Dream....................................... 197

ACKNOWLEDGMENTS

Thank you Jim.

Your faith, encouragement and inspiration gave me the
confidence to grow as a person and author.

I can never express how much I appreciate your
support and help to reach beyond my comfort zone and stretch
my abilities and dreams.

I love you.

INTRODUCTION

Are you looking to take your life to the next level? Do you have dreams but lack the motivation or discipline to achieve them? What is holding you back? These are some of the questions many of us wrestle with and sometimes we move to the next step or we stall and the things we want and dream of are just waiting until...

I get to a better place...

I can save up...

I finish...

We have many reasons to hold us back from life changes, but I believe you can develop, accomplish, reach and grow as a person.

Is it time for you to start on a journey to a new way of thinking?

This book is a collection of random thoughts looking at areas of life we juggle daily which touch us all in different ways.

By focusing on these areas, you can develop new skills to help you solve issues. Life is continual learning and by applying new actions or reactions to everyday life you can achieve balance and satisfaction for the future.

Are you ready to begin?

LEARN   GROW   ACHIEVE

This book is individual random thoughts written over several years. There is no order to these writings other than they touch on the eight areas of life I believe surround us daily. Each of these areas cover all aspects of our existence and daily decisions. The following are a few thoughts on each area of life.

Business and Career

We spend a majority of our time working on our business or career. We have education or training to be qualified but many times there are things blocking our success to reach beyond our current level.

Our expectations to be more profitable or advance to new positions are just beyond our grasp. What is holding you back? Is there something in your life that could unlock whatever is stopping you from moving up in your career? You may need to get out of your own way and learn the steps to get you to the next place in your profession.

Health and Wellness

Are you a living life to the fullest or are you on the road to a life of illness and pain? You don't have to be an Olympian or superstar to live well and healthy. You can change lifetime habits and feel better by taking care of yourself first. It's not all about diet and exercise. It's about what you are putting inside your head that can hurt you the most. You can take proactive steps to change your thoughts leading you to a future of better health.

Leadership and Performance
You don't have to be an entrepreneur or the company president to be a leader. Leadership is about caring for the people around you. Leaders give others the assurance they will take care of them. Leaders develop a culture of trust in their environment and accountability. They create great relationships with their teams, and clients that develop successful results and better connections.

Personal Development and Growth
Do you know what you value, have talent for, or can contribute to the world? Looking inside and finding these gems help you to grow and open new worlds to explore, gain knowledge and increase self-worth. Self-awareness and knowledge are powerful tools to increase your confidence in many areas of your life. You can change the things you don't like about yourself and grow as a person by knowing more about you, your talents and values.

Finance and Wealth
Have you created habits that are hurting you financially? Do you feel you are in this hole of debt and just can't get out? If you are spending more than you earn, then you should work on why the debt has gotten so out of control. Identifying your strengths and weaknesses in these areas can help get you on a better track to overcome poor financial habits. What are you doing to pay debt and have the freedom to live without worry?

Relationships
Life is surrounded by how we interact with others. Our business and personal life is a universe of give and take with the people we are involved with day to day.

Relationships take your life to the next level whether it's during a business negotiation or a friendship. Being able to build good relationships are paramount to achieving results and a better existence. Developing good communication, listening skills, with compassion and empathy for others, helps you understand more about yourself.

Fun, Adventure and Recreation
Play is important in all aspects of life. Humor, games and fun keeps us active and our mind sharp. Having fun in life gives us the downtime from our serious work and family commitments. It's needed to be creative, relieve stress and to improve relationships as well as energize you. Stepping outside of your comfort zone into the world of play and fun can give you the focus needed to prove yourself.

Learn what you need to recharge and give yourself a sense of freedom and enjoyment. It can lead you to the next step you want to achieve in your life.

Spiritual, Values and Community
These are the areas of our lives coming from a perspective within. Tapping into your deeper self will help you discover who you are, your values, life purpose and how you interact within your community.

Once you find out these important elements, you can make a shift in life to change course and move in a new direction discovering who you are and want to be.

Knowing who you are and what you truly value in life will help you become a more cherished and respected partner, parent, team player and leader within your world.

These different areas play a part in our life every day. This book of random thoughts gives perspective on how we can live each day making the most of life and focus on improving our self.

Here we go.

CHANGING

I have spent a life-time facing change. Many times I have embraced the adjustment and sometimes I have been dragged into it kicking and screaming. Most often when I have resisted change it turned out to be the best thing for me. Whether you are shifting where you live, altering your career, or who is in your life; change can be a wonderful experience. We only need to open our eyes to see what it brings to us. It's all about attitude and focus.

I remember when I moved to the Middle East back in the 1980's. This was a huge change for a small-town Missouri girl who had only flown twice in her life. Although I feared the unknown, I was also excited to explore a new world. What I discovered from this experience is people overall react to change differently. They either embrace change and learn from it or reject it and hide.

I still have fears but now know change can bring good things to me. I look for new and different encounters that will enrich my life. Whether it's going back to school, changing relationships, or moving into a new area; it's not about the change itself, but how you look and accept it into your life.

Learning to welcome change can be difficult. Your thoughts when something new didn't work out as planned can make all the difference in how you feel about the experience. Are you thinking it was a waste of time or not worth the effort? Or are you seeing how the experience taught you something and enriched your life? I have been down many paths that didn't always work out as planned, but learned and gained skills that continued with me to this day.

We have constant change in our lives. We gain and lose businesses, homes, jobs, friends and family members. It's not easy and, yes, sometimes it does feels like rocket science. If you want to live and not just exist, then change will be in your life. Are you letting life pass you by or are you making things happen? We get to choose how we think and accept the adjustments in our life. Are you resisting or are you growing?

PAST, PRESENT AND FUTURE

Is it time for a career and business checkup? Take a moment to look at what you have done, where you are now, and what you can do going forward. The following ideas can apply to your personal and professional life.

What can you do to prepare for the future? Here are my top ten ideas:

10) Take a look at the last year and make a note of what worked and what failed. Don't repeat the same mistakes.

9) You don't need "word of mouth," you need "right word of mouth." Make sure you are getting the right word. People with a bad experience will spread the word much faster than those with a good experience. How do you provide a good experience?

8) Value is everything. Are you giving good value? Individuals need a reason to buy even "on-sale" items.

7) Customer service. This will make or break a business. Great customer service will result in returning customers and they will tell others to use your business.

6) Be authentic. People are smart. You can't fake it.

5) Mix it up. Are you doing, displaying, or marketing the same items, message, etc. as you were last year? Change the look, message, or display. Take a lesson from the big stores and give customers a reason to check and see what you are doing now, today.

4) Tell the world what makes you unique. Why should they buy from you and not someone else?

3) Are you tracking where your clients come from and what brought them to you?

2) Watch for cross promotion opportunities with a related industry. You can add new patrons and develop new business relationships.

1) Be positive. People like and are attracted to positive people.

THE LITTLE THINGS IN LIFE

When my dearest friend and sister passed away I was shocked and surprised by her death. I was not ready to think about her no longer being available for advice, a laugh, a secret, or just a hello. Losing someone dear to your heart will make you think about life and the meaning.

One important thing I have learned and keep foremost in my mind is to appreciate the "little things in life."

In this crazy, fast pace world we are always on the move, getting information and looking for the next fad to fulfill our needs. But do we see the little things daily that are the miracles in our lives? Here are a few things I have come to appreciate, and I am sure you will have many more to add to the list once you think about it for yourself.

Breathing- Each day I am thankful that I have another day to enjoy. I, unlike many in my family, don't have problems with asthma, lung disease, or breathing. I can enjoy each day.

Movement- I am a healthy person and able to do many things. I appreciate that I can be lazy but I keep moving and doing things in life I want to do.

Freedom to choose- Whether it's learning something new, where to work, travel, home, or change my beliefs, I can choose what I want or need.

Nature- I can enjoy a sunrise or beautiful sunset. I can watch the world work it miracles through nature and how it all revolves in a circle. The most precious art is the world around us.

Smiles- Whether it's the twinkle in the eyes of my husband or the shy smile of a child, I receive this gift and enjoy them. I try to remember to give as many smiles as I receive.

People- The special ones in my life who are friends, mentors, and family. I appreciate them all and that I am a part of their life.

The bottom line is to be thankful, happy and cherish the connections you have today. Take a moment to note the *"little things in life"* because most of them are not little at all.

"True greatness consists in being great in little things," **-Charles Simmons**

THE MESSAGES YOU ARE SENDING

The world has changed from the days we wrote formal letters and thank you notes to our business partners, family and friends. Today, it is rare to receive a letter or card in the mail with a personal message. I am guilty of this too. I find it easier to type an email rather than handwrite a note. Plus, I will send an e-card rather than a card purchased from a store. The point is I, like many of you, have moved into the digital world and find good and bad with the results.

Our standards and expectations have changed. We can write an email or text rather than make a phone call. We communicate through machines and live somewhat in a virtual world. Some of us have issues or difficulty with the new ways of communication. I find you can have the best of both worlds if a little common sense is used.

Are you sending out the right messages? Do you think about how your communication is received? If we get down to the basics, you will find communication is about a relationship with others. Are you building good relationships? Is the receiver of your messages feeling understood, important, and valued?

How your messages are perceived is important, whether it pertains to your personal or business life.

So, here are ideas to think about that may help you create better relationships:

Trust is the most important thing you can do to create strong relationships. There are people you know whose only interest is **what's in it for me.** Others are just the opposite. They are going above and beyond to create that trust. They are truthful without trying to gain from the relationship.

Giving people value creates strong relationships. That old saying of treating others as you like to be treated is still true.

Recognizing other's strengths and complimenting them shows you are paying attention and giving their efforts value. And remember, saying the occasional thank you will go a long way too. I have worked with people who made me feel I was an important part of a team effort. I have also worked with people who made me feel my efforts were unimportant and they could not care less. I am sure you can imagine how people react to each of those types of situations and the effort they put into going above and beyond.

To end these thoughts, I give you the *Ten Commandments of Good Human Relations* by Robert G. Lee:

10 Commandments of Human Relations

1. **Speak to people**. There is nothing as nice as a cheerful word of greeting.
2. **Smile at people**. It takes 72 muscles to frown, only 14 to smile.
3. **Call people by name**. The sweetest music to anyone's ears is the sound of his own name.

4. **Be friendly and helpful**. If you want friends, you must be one.
5. **Be cordial**. Speak and act as if everything you do is a joy to you.
6. **Be genuinely interested in people**. You can like almost everybody if you try.
7. **Be generous with praise**... and cautious with criticisms.
8. **Be considerate with the feelings of others**. There are usually three sides to a controversy: Yours, the other fellow's and the right side.
9. **Be eager to lend a helping hand**. Often it is appreciated more than you know.
10. Add to this: **a good sense of humor, a huge dose of patience and a dash of humility**.

LISTEN TO YOUR GUT

Do you occasionally just know something you can't quite explain? It's a feeling or instinct that turns out to be right. It has been called *listening to your gut* or *gut instinct*. Listening to your gut can work well for you. I bet you know the feeling. It is a snap decision you sense is right. It's a warning telling you to be careful, to take a moment, to avoid a person or situation. Those gut feelings aren't always exact, but are worth taking time to note. We have natural intuition, but don't always trust or pay attention to those feelings.

We are not always in tune with our self or surroundings. More often, we are either too trustful or don't pay attention to what is going on around us. Are you aware of your surroundings? Being alert can help you in many areas of your life. If you are conscious of other people's actions and motives, it will help you better understand your involvement with them.

Listen to that little voice inside you. It's important to trust yourself. There is a source telling you why you are having these feelings. Most of it is coming from your subconscious and all your previous experiences. Scientists have discovered through research that our unconscious mind can influence our behaviors and goals.

Our brain and intuition act from experiences. Being able to decipher what is real can help you make better decisions.

Become a people watcher. Pay attention to your surroundings. You can learn so much by just being observant. Details are important. Analyze your daily situations. Stick to the facts and not what you want to believe. Learn to read people and their motives. For example, is their actions caused by greed, power, or control? Are you open to the possibilities or are you seeing what you want to believe? Remember you can always talk with a trusted person about your conclusions. Feedback can help you gain trust in your instincts.

Whether you are starting a relationship, purchasing a big ticket item, or playing a game, using your gut can be helpful. But, remember it is only one of your tools in making life decisions.

"Experience taught me a few things. One is to listen to your gut, no matter how good something sounds on paper. The second is that you're generally better off sticking with what you know. And the third is that sometimes your best investments are the ones you don't make." - Donald Trump

MOUNTAIN OF LESSONS

Several years ago, I was on the adventure of a lifetime. At the time, I didn't realize how it would impact my outlook on life but, looking back, I see many lessons from that trip. I, along with eleven other people, was on the quest to climb Mt. Kilimanjaro. This 19,341-foot mountain is in Tanzania, Africa. It is the highest mountain in Africa and the highest free-standing mountain in the world. The terrain on Kilimanjaro falls into very clear categories. Lower altitudes are forest, the middle is heather, and moorland, and top is basically desert. The beginning of the trip at the base of the mountain is humid, warm tropical weather. As you work your way up the mountain, it becomes colder and then freezing when you reach the summit and the glacier.

Our group was on a nine-day trek to reach the top and return to the base. Surprisingly, we had forty porters, two assistant guides and one head guide to help the group on the trip. Climbing Kilimanjaro takes a village. You may not realize it, but for a trip of this magnitude, everything must be carried with you. Think about that for a minute. These porters carried all the tents, food, water, tables, chairs, cooking gear, sleeping bags, and many other items. These very thin and incredibly strong people carried an average of 40-50 pounds on their heads. Tanzania is a very poor country and these porters are happy and grateful to have their jobs.

Unbelievably, many of the porters that work on the mountain treks will complete one trip, turn around, and start another.

Okay, back to the lessons learned on the trip. First is the lesson of getting along for the common good. When you have that many people on the side of a mountain, you don't always see things the same way. You have personality differences, but you learn to keep going forward and get along.

The second lesson is group support. Each day is a challenge for someone in the group. It may be a slight disability or a major fear, but the group encourages each other to continue. They laugh, cry and watch out for potential problems. They are patient with the slowest one in the group and happy for any rest breaks along the way.

Third is gratitude. You welcome each day when the porters have broken camp that morning and pass you on the trail to set up at the next location. With thanks, you are greeted with a warm meal and drink from the people that are supporting you throughout the trip. Seeing a sunrise or sunset from a different level on the mountain each day opens your eyes to the beauty of our world. You appreciate the wonders our earth provides.

Fourth is finding trust and faith in yourself. You have faith you will continue and trust your boots will hold where you place your foot. You continue to think you will acclimate to the altitude and not be reduced to the sickness that has turn back many just before the summit.

Fifth is having empathy for others. You find empathy for others when you see the pain of defeat in those who fail to reach the top of the mountain. In your heart, you know it could have been you.

The final lesson is survival and focus. Each day is a survival. The long daily hikes, not bathing, the difficulty breathing thin air, and enduring the cold teaches inner strength. The goal is to complete the trip - period. You find faith in yourself, as well as faith, trust, and the good in others. You understand what you are made of and how much you really can tolerate and still move forward.

What a great learning experience and adventure! These are lessons I will carry with me for the rest of my life. Look for the lessons you can carry with you.

SMALL CHANGES CAN BRING BIG CHANGE

Many of us wait for the New Year as an opportunity to start over and change our lives. We do this by setting goals, making resolutions, or a promise to ourselves. It's all with good intentions and planning may even be part of the process. The problem occurs when we apply these changes into the everyday pattern of our life.

Let me tell you that *change* is hard. It's *uncomfortable*.

To stick to your plan is more difficult because, most times, you don't have support. The world is working against you much of the time. For example, do you find that all kinds of things can creep into your life if your goal is get daily exercise? It could be family obligations, work or many other types of distractions, but the end result is you don't follow through with your plan.

Another example is healthier eating and losing those extra pounds. How many times has someone said to you, "Oh go ahead, one bite will not hurt you." I feel you nodding your head at that one.

So, do you give up and blame your family, surroundings, or work environment and quit? Hopefully not. I have found I have to need or want something very badly to make a change. It must be important enough to not give in to excuses. The result needs to drive me to continue until the habit it formed.

You may need to plan. If you want to exercise, plan when you can do that and then have a backup plan. If you want to eat better, write down a weekly menu and buy those items.

Want to be more organized? Then work on a daily list and put items in places where you will look for them. Whatever your goal, plan for it, then make it part of your daily routine. The daily routine is the hard part of this change. Habits take time, so don't be discouraged.

A piece of advice; don't change everything at once. I heard a term that I really like. It's called "single-tasking." Opposite of "multi-tasking." It means to focus on one thing and do it well. Make your list with the details of what you want to accomplish, but focus on one item at a time. You will not be so overwhelmed and you will be setting yourself up for success.

If you are still feeling overwhelmed and cannot get a habit created, then think smaller. For example, if your goal is to be more organized then start with putting one thing in its place. It could be placing your keys in the same place every day or throwing papers in the recycle bin rather than leaving a pile on the table.

Finally, reward yourself for your accomplishments. Don't think you must wait until you reach the final goal. Every day pat yourself on the back for the smallest accomplishment. Do a little happy dance for saying *"YES"* to the smallest change. You and only you oversee these tiny choices for change in your life.

"The 3 C's of life: choices, chances and changes. You must make a choice to take a chance or your life will never change." - Unknown

ROBIN ANNE GRIFFITHS

WHAT OTHERS CAN TEACH US

- A co-worker smiled at me and said, "I decided to be happy and although I don't feel it yet, I will fake it until I make it."

- I had a sales training day and my trainee was more interested in telling me what is wrong with the company rather than learning how it works, then help make suggestions.

- I have an acquaintance that always needs the center of attention and has created a world to get that attention.

- I have a cousin that glows of inner peace and always turn a comment into something positive.

- My husband is always working to improve the world around him to be better, more efficient, and practical.

- I know a person who enjoys gaining support by gossiping.

- A friend of mine is always finding a new challenge to overcome and improve her life.

- There is a person in my life that has great challenges and never complains.

- A life coach helped me understand that ninety-seven percent of what bothers us is not important and taught me to find the three percent that is important. Let the other stuff go.

Be aware how your words and actions can affect others. What are you teaching the people in your life? Are you showing your children a positive, honest, trustworthy parent? What type of thoughts and encouragement do you give to the people around you? Are you a good example?

It's so easy to fall into the negative world. And I believe it can be contagious. It's a disease we carry and pass on from person to person unless we decide to stop and change our focus. I don't believe this means you need to move into an unrealistic lifestyle. Perhaps a little change here and there will give you a new direction and have a major impact on another's life. A good way to start each morning is with gratefulness. We are so focused on what we don't have, we forget to give thanks for all the wonderful things we do have.

Think about the type of person you want to be to others. I read an article - *It Started With*, by Sarah Kathleen Peck, which shared the different energy personalities people exhibit. She talked about three different groups: The Positives, The Middle Balance and the Negatives.

The Positives types are upbeat, inspirational, coaches or mentors in life. The Middle Balance are the stabilizers, feedback providers, or people working towards change, and on a path to become the person they want to be. Finally, the Negatives are the non-changers, have negative influences and are toxic to be around.

The most important part of this article was not if these people are good or bad, but how they make you feel.

My final question for you is how are the people in your life making you feel and what are you projecting and making them feel? Put a little thought into that and it may change your life.

"Attitude is a choice. Happiness is a choice. Optimism is a choice. Kindness is a choice. Giving is a choice. Respect is a choice. Whatever choice you make makes you. Choose wisely." – Roy T. Bennett, The Light in the Heart

SAYING I DID IT

My friends and family know I have been on a quest for the past several years to write a book about my mother's life. Born in 1922 she lived for ninety-one years. Imagine the changes she saw in her lifetime!

This mission was not an easy task, and I worked on it in the quiet early morning over several years. It was a quest, a dream, healing therapy and, ultimately part of my routine and life.

The project had become something I felt compelled to do and accomplish. Finally, I finished the manuscript and sent it off to my editor. It was an emotional moment knowing I did it. I completed something I had been talking about for a long time.

The book had become part of my everyday existence and it was ready for the next step and I can move on to the next goal in my life. What a feeling!

Do you have a dream? Is there a little thought in the back of your mind just waiting to be brought to life but has not been put into action?

I have found most people fall into two categories when it comes to things they want to do - they either talk about it or make it become a reality.

Mostly when these ideas, dreams, or goals are not moved to the next step it's because of fear or not a true goal. A friend may talk about living and traveling by boat to see the world, but doesn't move forward with the idea. It's just talk. Many of us do that because at that moment it sounds interesting, romantic, adventurous, or fun. We have no intentions of taking any steps towards accomplishing such a great adventure.

But there are dreams, thoughts and, ideas you would like to do but are at a loss of what steps to take. You don't move forward because of a fear you won't be able to accomplish the task. Or perhaps you are just putting it off until the mysterious day that will give you the time to do all the things you have set aside.

My advice to you is stop waiting and start doing. Start by thinking of ways that will motivate you to move forward.

Give yourself goals and rewards for achieving them. Set goals that are smart and doable. This could mean changing your daily routine. I got up early so I could write in the morning for about an hour. Find a time that works for you and it becomes a habit. Then put it in writing and make a plan you can follow.

I had an end date based on how much and often I was writing. The manuscript was finished a month later than planned but I still felt it was on track. I also did not have unrealistic ideas of what I could do, so it took the stress and pressure off.

Most of all, you need to stick with it. You may have delays, but if you have a plan, you will get back on track more easily.

Finally, you will want to communicate to others what you are doing to gain support. They can be your cheerleaders for motivation and encouragement, but remember that this is something you are doing for you.

So go out there and get busy so you can pat yourself on the back and say, "I did it!"

"If your dreams don't scare you, they aren't big enough." - Unknown

GETTING WHAT YOU WANT

I was listening to a teleconference on confidence and how we sabotage ourselves into believing things that are not true. Some people look at themselves as a victim or they don't act on something they feel is important because of fear.

Low self-confidence or self-esteem can be the culprit for the behavior. Often, we will not take risk because of fear.

Are there items on your bucket list you don't believe will ever happen? Perhaps you are feeling defeated because you haven't been able to get that one thing you have wanted. You may feel there is always something stopping you from accomplishing your dream.

Why do we have these road blocks keeping us from getting what we say we want? Are we stopping ourselves from getting success? There may be several barriers keeping us from what we want.

One reason may be you don't believe you deserve to get (pick all that apply) happiness, love, success, money, or career. You live in a bubble of protection, don't take risk, put others' needs first or just don't want to rock the boat.

Here are a few thoughts that may ring true if you are looking but not getting what you want in life.

I have been in sales and marketing for many years and found most people don't get a sale or anything else because they just don't ask. They may believe they are worthy for whatever they want from another person or company. They simply don't ask for fear of rejection.

What do you believe is the worst that can happen if you pursue what you want? Knowing what may happen based on the worst can help you better prepare. You may attain what you want just by asking.

Another example why we don't get what we want is we don't try. I have friends that want to run, lose weight, find the right relationship or learn a new skill, but they always have an excuse why they can't accomplish the feat.

The excuses don't matter. They don't try because they have already decided they can't achieve their goal.

Did you want it? A life coach told me once that focus is the key to getting what you want. Find the one thing you really want and work on it. Before you know it, you have attained that important item and then can move onto the next.

If you think about that for a moment, you will see when you are trying to juggle multiple desires many or all can fall. Bottom line - focus on what you really want.

Perhaps you are not sure what you want. Sometimes we don't have a clue how important something can be until we have experienced it.

I would recommend you keep an open mind and see what is out there and available.

You may be surprised where it leads you and how it changes your perspective.

"Never let life impede on your ability to manifest your dreams. Dig deeper into your dreams and deeper into yourself and believe that anything is possible, and make it happen." - Corin Nemec

LEADING AND INSPIRING

I watched an interview with Simon Sinek, author, speaker, and consultant on leadership and management. He was talking about leadership and how to inspire others to do remarkable things. His thought is a great way to look at how we interact with others, whether they be our friends, family, coworkers or customers. One of his points was how to create a safe environment where people wake up every day inspired to go to work. He added people should feel fulfilled by their work and their contribution to something greater than themselves.

Hmmm, I wonder how many people out there are looking to be inspired, care about the work they do, or the relationships they have with others. Then I realized, when it comes right down to it, you know if you are doing the right thing. Other opinions aren't important. It's about knowing you are doing the best you can to make life a better place for you and others.

So often the public thinks of leaders as the head of a company, government, or a person in a high position. Contrary to that belief, a leader can be your parent, an employee, or a friend. It can be anyone.

Let's look at the qualities that define a leader. Leaders understand that it's not about them. They get it. Leaders take care of others and have selflessness in their character. They also have a way of developing trust, have empathy, and put others ahead of themselves. Good leaders know their purpose but also can communicate it to others. Speaking of communicating, leaders know communication isn't about talking but about listening. Good leaders are like parents, they protect others by taking the risk and they make sacrifices so the people important to them are safe. This is a phenomenon because the effect of a good leader will make people give their all to see their leaders' vision come to life.

Leadership is a learned skill and by taking the time to find out what kind of person you are you can then take steps to become the person you want to be.

"If your actions inspire others to dream more, learn more, do more and become more, you are a leader." -John Quincy Adams

THRIVING NOT JUST SURVIVING

During the process of writing a book about my mother's life, it hit me how much I learned from her without even realizing it. She was a very strong individual without knowing it herself. She was a survivor, but even more, she lived life. Here are a few of the lessons she taught me:

Do your best and keep going. We find many obstacles in our way as we move along day to day. Sometimes they can overwhelm us and make us stall. Don Miguel Ruiz tells us that our best is not always the same, but to work always towards it. Some days your best will vary depending on your health, mood, or other factors. If you continually strive to do your best, you develop a habit and your best continues to improve. My mother always looked back on the decisions she made with the thought she did her best and I don't believe she had many regrets.

Don't be afraid to try new things. I believe we stop short of living life to our fullest by fear of the unknown. Fear can help us with boundaries but so often we let it hold us from reaching our full potential. Doubt and worry can overcome us and prevent us from pursuing our dreams and life-fulfilling moments. Fear can hold us back from living a bolder life. My mother was fearful of many things. One fear was water as she never learned to swim. That didn't stop her from getting on the water to experience new and different adventures. One of her proudest moments was getting on a Catamaran in Hawaii with a group of people and her young grandchildren. She was terrified to be on the back of the open vessel as it moved out into the swells of the ocean, waves splashing up over the sides. Her thoughts at that moment were if anything happen she could not help her two grandsons since she did not swim. Afterward she looked back at the experience as a lifetime adventure she would have not missed.

Make friends and keep them close. Friends bring richness to your life and a true friend can bring you a lifetime of value. Cultivate true friends and learn the value of what you can do for them. Friends can help you when you are in need but, more than that, they are the sounding board for thoughts and balance. My mother had a multitude of friends. She had over two hundred in attendance at her eightieth birthday party to help her celebrate. She developed friendships and kept them over a lifetime.

Keep learning. Life learning is more than school or picking up a new hobby. It is more about keeping an open mind to new experiences. It's about exploring possibilities and looking beyond your comfortable space. My mother was a lifelong learner. She loved to read. Her reading took her to different places and opened her mind to different ideas and thoughts about life. She experienced so much change in her ninety-one years. Other than refusing to use a computer, she was open to learning and trying new things as the world changed.

We need to keep an open mind and look at the lessons we can take with us to build a better and more successful life. We need to look out beyond our daily habits and reach for more experiences, friends and life celebrations. There is no test other than knowing you did your best to live your life to the fullest.

"It's not about what you tell your children, but how you show them how to live life." - Jada Pinkett Smith

"Somebody should tell us, right at the start of our lives, that we are dying. Then we might live life to the limit, every minute of every day. Do it! I say. Whatever you want to do, do it now! There are only so many tomorrows." -Pope Paul VI

IN AND OUT OF BALANCE

Having balance in your life is important. That means finding time for yourself. It doesn't matter if you work for a large corporation, a small mom and pop, or for yourself as an entrepreneur, having balance in your life is crucial.

So, what does that mean? Taking care of yourself and the loved ones in your life means different things to each individual. You alone can look at your life and decide what will give you balance. Are you in tune with what is going on in your life and how it is affecting you and others? I know a few people that are so passionate about their goals they run themselves to exhaustion trying to achieve the impossible. I also know others that are scared, worried and distracted by so many things in their lives they are virtually chasing themselves and accomplishing little. So where does this crazy non-stop, ongoing quest to do everything end? And how do you create balance and achieve your best?

Here are a few things that may help you find balance, bring you comfort, rest, and more success in your future.

First, do you find time to disconnect from the job or people? I have a friend that starts the day reading a chapter from something inspiring. Another friend writes while another uses yoga and meditation to start the day.

Don't think you have time? Then look at what you are currently doing to see what you may change. Can you make arrangements to work in some time for you? Perhaps you can say no to something you are now doing. Think how important it is to reboot and give yourself the needed moments for more life enjoyment.

Remember, you are the only person who can give permission to take care of you. Begin by writing down actions that will help nurture you. Maybe it's spending time alone reading, walking, running, crafting, fishing, or listening to music. Are you taking care of yourself inside? Are you eating well, getting enough exercise and rest? You may not be able or want to join a gym, but you can make small decisions each day that lead to a better and healthier lifestyle.

What are your priorities? It is so easy to get immersed in a multitude of things that appear to take on a lives of their own. Before you realize it every minute of your day is filled with all kinds of projects that must be done. Decisions can be made to help guide you from falling into that abyss. Look for what is significate and how it will affect others.

Are you planning your day and organizing what is most important? You can achieve more and not waste time with a clear plan or road map guiding you. Benjamin Franklin said it best when he talked about how we don't plan to fail, but certainly fail to plan. Make a to-do list, write things on a calendar, and schedule your recreation and quality time.

You will still have detours along the way, but don't be discouraged. It is much easier to pick up where you left off when the unexpected happens. This happens because you have a direction to refer to and get yourself back on track.

Simplify your life. See what you have too much of and cut out the excess. Look for simplicity in your work, relationships, and exposure to the outside world.

Bringing your life into balance can create joy, happiness and peace. Put time and effort into looking at where you want to be and move in that direction.

"Just as your car runs more smoothly and requires less energy to go faster and farther when the wheels are in perfect alignment, you perform better when your thoughts, feelings, emotions, goals, and values are in balance." - Brian Tracy

HOW'S THAT WORKING OUT?

Many of you have heard Dr. Phil's coined phrase, "So how's that working out for you?" Have you thought for a moment about what you are doing? A good friend reminded me of Albert Einstein's theory on getting results. Einstein said, "Doing things the same way you always have and expecting the results to be different is insanity."

When I am assessing the past and where I want to be, I look to see if I have landed in a rut. Am I working for results without changing the route to get there?

Ask yourself, " Am I in a comfort zone?" I am referring to the easy path. It's easy to fall into and many times it will cause us not to achieve the results we are wanting. Life is complex and we face many challenges. Sometimes we forget to look at the big picture. We keep doing the same thing over and over for a variety of reasons or excuses.

What were your goals last year? Are any of these familiar? Lose weight, stick to a budget, eliminate debt, spend more time with love ones, find a soul mate, quit smoking, get a better job, learn something new, volunteer, and become organized. Many of these are common objectives but just don't get done. What percentage of completion did you achieve this past year? Were you doing business as usual hoping that you'll get lucky and a miracle will magically give you results?

If you are you wanting to achieve a personal or business goal, then perhaps it's time to move in a new direction. Are you willing to make sacrifices to achieve your vision? Change is hard, but the rewards can be great. Stop the insanity and ACT!

Make a list and plan how to get what you want with a due date. Say it out loud. Tell your family, friends, and business associates what you are working towards. Get help. There are all kinds of resources to help you. You can get help from books, internet, acquaintances, and organizational services to name a few.

You don't have to recreate the wheel either. Planning and follow through is where the rubber meets the road. You can start a plan whether you want to run a marathon, climb a mountain, increase your sales, create better customer service, make a better product or just lose ten pounds. Each day look at your list and take steps to get what you want. Be patient. Results takes time, but each day you will move forward and make changes.

Keep the good. Evaluate what is working and continue, but if it's not working, Einstein would say you need to do something different. You can set your expectations for results and be creative on how to reach them. Plan now to stretch out of that comfort zone and change your life so you stop the insanity.

CHANGING YOUR ATTITUDE

I have been reading about attitude and how we respond and express ourselves within different environments. Attitude can make a big difference in all aspects of our lives. It's easy to have a positive attitude when life is going well, but as daily living gets tougher, we need to stop and see how we are reacting. Having a negative attitude will hold consequences. People do not want to be around a person who can suck all the good out of the air and that is what a negative attitude will do.

Many of us are dealing with new and different pressures we didn't have a few years ago. How are you handling that pressure? Are you fearful, angry, and sad? Although you may not be saying it out loud, your family, friends, and business acquaintances can likely sense and recognize it. Maybe you're not satisfied and believe things could be better. If so, then look at positive actions you can take. Changing an attitude can alter the way the world is viewed.

You have the power to change your attitude and the way you view life. A good start is to assess what it is you need to adjust. What is the underlying reason for your negative attitude? Set goals that will help you change. Change can be difficult - and if you dwell on the struggle, it will be! Don't fear mistakes and take risks. Use the word **yet**. Instead of *"I can't figure it out"* use *"I haven't figure it out **yet** but I will."* That little three letter word has the power to change your negative attitude into opportunity thinking. Keep looking at what you are trying to achieve and think about the rewards of what you are working toward. Remember giving your best will leave you with no regrets. Don't make excuses, make progress. Accept responsibility and show gratitude for the chance to be better at life.

"Realize that if you have time to whine and complain about something then you have the time to do something about it." - Anthony J. D'Angelo

FIND THE PERFECT FIT

I spend a lot of time writing about business strategies and work, but a part of your business life is keeping a balance with your family, friends, and sanity.

On a fishing trip, I thought about my father who loved the outdoors. He was hunting or fishing at every opportunity that presented itself. He was an independent painter and wallpaper hanger with little education who had to hustle to find work. His hours were long and his work was hard labor, but he found enjoyment in his craft. He also found time to enjoy his pleasures which were hunting with his dogs, fishing for his food, and watching or listening to baseball.

Thinking about dad made me realize how important it is to have balance in your life. If your life is out of balance, stress levels may run high. Finding that balance in today's frenetically paced world is no simple task. I believe we all want and need to have a good balance with work, family, friends, health and fun. Most of all we need to be on guard how work invades into our personal life and the effect it has on each of us.

Because of instant communication with mobile phones and email, our professional life can creep into our personal life. We feel fatigued and we miss out on important events with our family or friends due to the increasing daily demands. It's very challenging and difficult to strike a balance, especially if you own your own business.

Find more balance with leaving work at work. Next, learn to say no if you tend to over-obligate yourself. It's fine to say no. When you quit saying yes for the things you do only out of guilt or a false sense of obligation, you will find room for more important events you want.

Try to better manage your time. Keep a calendar that includes everyone important in your family. Set aside time to nurture yourself and unwind whether it's going to the gym, reading, or a bubble bath. If you have a day off protect it. Get enough sleep. Use your trusted friendships to help in times of stress or hardship.

Creating balance in your life is a continuous process. Demands on your time change as your family, interests and work change. Assess your situation every few months to make sure you're on track. Balance doesn't mean doing everything. It means you are finding a middle ground that works for you. Only you can restore harmony and peace to your life.

POSITIVE PROBLEMS

Do you believe you have problems? Many of us think we do. How many times do you hear, *"We have a problem,"* or *"We need to solve a problem."* The usage of any of the following words also applies: difficulty, bad situation, can of worms, complication, dilemma, disagreement, dispute, issue, obstacle, predicament, quandary, and trouble.

Problems creep into our everyday life so how we handle them is important. Many of us don't want to deal with them or we will deny they exist.

I believe how we handle or look at problems controls much of our outlook on life and how we live. It comes down to asking yourself the right questions and looking for true answers. If you can be honest with yourself and find answers, you will then look at your problem in a different light. You can change your approach which then will change your outcome.

The idea is to focus on the solution rather than the problem itself. Asking yourself the right questions taps into your subconscious mind.

For example, if you ask yourself a negative question, your brain will come up with reasons to answer that question. This is of no help and your brain is confirming what you asked. Instead ask yourself a positive question. An example of a negative question such as, *"Why do I always fail?"* can be changed to, *"How can I learn from this?"*

Your brain will look for a strategy to help you learn. The brain will always present an answer to any question you ask yourself. It feels obligated to respond to your questions even though the answer may not be necessarily true. Train yourself to ask only positive questions such as, "How can I succeed in this venture?"

Simple questions have powerful effects. Begin a habit of asking yourself positive based questions and look for the opportunities to learn from your experiences.

"Most people never feel secure because they are always worried that they will lose their job, lose the money they already have, lose their spouse, lose their health, and so on. The only true security in life comes from knowing that every single day you are improving yourself in some way, that you are increasing the caliber of who you are and that you are valuable to your company, your friends, and your family." – Anthony Robbins

WHAT DID YOU SAY?

Okay, I admit it. I have a communication problem. I don't always hear what is said; or I misinterpret what was said. I wasn't listening attentively. I think I know what you will say instead of what you are telling me. And, worst of all, I don't always communicate what needs to be said because I want to avoid conflict. Please don't take it personally, I have a communication disorder! I don't always listen and I don't always communicate what I mean. Please don't laugh as it can be a real problem and cause major conflict. I am working on improving my listening and communication skills. If you have some of these same issues the following ideas that may help you too.

You may think communicating is not that hard to do. But effective communication is an art and takes practice. Our world has added so many new ways to communicate. With these advancements we have also lost some of the basic techniques. Add that to individual personalities and before you know it, just talking to each other can be unbelievably difficult. How many times have you read an email, talked to a person or listened to a news report and felt confused, upset, or excessively happy? It is likely that you have been subjected to miscommunication.

Miscommunication can be funny, but also dangerous, and even

tragic. Think how important communication is with soldiers on the battlefield, air traffic controllers, or even medical teams in hospitals. We communicate more than ever digitally in today's environment. I have received emails with demands in bold red type and all capital letters. Have you ever felt like someone is screaming at you in an email? My point is effective communication is complicated.

When you are having an issue with communication, remain focused. Stay in the present and work to understand. Listen carefully. Don't drift. I am sure many of us can relate to the following example: You are talking to someone and you lose interest. Before you know it, your mind is elsewhere. At that exact moment, the other person ask a question or wants agreement and you have no idea what was just said. People often think they're listening. In fact, they are thinking about what they are going to say next when the other person stops talking. Truly effective communication goes both ways. While it might be difficult, try listening to what the other person is saying. Don't interrupt. Don't get defensive. Just hear them and reflect on what they are saying so they know you have heard them. You'll understand them better and they will be more willing to listen to you. Others are more likely to listen if they feel they are being heard.

Another communication issue is during the giving or receiving of criticism. When communicating, feelings can be bruised and defenses go up. While criticism is hard to hear, and often exaggerated by emotions, it's important to listen. Remember, manners count. People feel at ease and more receptive to what you say when you are polite. Using the word "I" lets people know you are saying something that is only according to your personal understanding, not a blanket fact. This keeps people from feeling targeted or attacked. There's a difference between telling someone, *"You're ignoring me,"* and *"I feel you are ignoring me."* Emphasize the positive. A positive tone will allow people to be freer to listen and prevents them from feeling defensive.

Be actively listening to the conversation. Engage your brain in the subject. Avoid using vocabulary that people won't understand or general terms that will leave people confused. Anticipate reactions, but never assume you know how someone will react.

Finally, patience is a virtue for effective communication. If you rush things and become frustrated, your communication abilities suffer. If you are always ready to slow the pace as needed or go back over certain points, you will communicate much more effectively. Thanks for listening and I hope I have communicated this well!

FIRST IMPRESSIONS ARE LASTING IMPRESSIONS

I walked into a business and assumptions were made about who I was and why I was there. Because of their actions I will never do business there again. That first impression will forever affect my feelings.

Involvements like this can brand a business and determine how people share their experiences. Events will begin by a few actions that cause a chain of reactions. Think about that for a moment and how it can affect you.

Have you called or gone into a business and the first person you meet had a bad attitude, was rude, or seemed too busy to acknowledge you? Or did you get profiled because of how you looked? A first impression is lasting. A bad start can happen by not being greeted or acknowledged and gives the impression of an unhappy business.

Businesses put a lot of time and effort into logos, ad designs, store displays, and other material things. I often wonder how much time is spent on educating the staff about helping the people that keep the business open and pay the salaries.

People look and develop an impression about you in a matter of seconds. They will judge your business in many ways: cleanliness, knowledge, helpfulness, responsiveness, and understanding. That first impression will have a tremendous impact and determine if they like, dislike or are indifferent to you.

Here are a few thoughts to see if you are creating a good first impression:

Greet the person. Always make eye contact even if you are with another individual or on the phone. Acknowledge them immediately. Smile! A friendly greeting disarms the person and sets them at ease. If they have an appointment and they are early, don't communicate this is a problem.

Don't have personal conversations or phone calls while meeting. Let them know they have your full attention.

Don't talk about anything negative including staff, other clients or competitors.

Don't express an attitude of being too busy or overworked. You may be very busy but your customers don't want to hear it, and it gives an impression they are adding to your stress.

Stay off your phone, social media and don't answer emails. It can wait. People contact you because they want to work with you. Start out with a good impression and people will say good things about you.

You never get a second chance to make a first impression." – Unknown

AGGRAVATION!

I am frustrated. I feel this way now and then. This happens when I am trying to accomplish something and it's just not working out as planned. Most often I am impatient and have this need for something to happen immediately.

We are a society of immediate satisfaction. Our attention span has diminished with fast food, express lanes, call waiting, instant text messages and speed dial. How many times have you been in a line at the bank or in the store and people are angry because it's not moving quickly enough? Do you get a little road rage when traffic is moving slowly?

Frustration not only happens in our personal lives, but our professional lives too. It could be a business deal that is not closing. You are not receiving replies to emails or phone messages and jobs are just not getting done as fast as you want or need. Perhaps you feel you are spinning your wheels and just want to give up. So how do you deal with the frustration and turn it around to your advantage?

The best place to start is to stop and reevaluate. Ask yourself, "What is working?" Sometimes we get so caught up in what is not working we lose the big picture and forget the positive things that are taking place. Look again at what you are trying to accomplish over all. Don't get so focused you lose sight of the goal.

Perhaps just being able to vent will help release some of the negative energy. You can scream into a pillow or my favorite; a silent scream in a locked room. Even more helpful is to verbalize your frustration to someone who will be supportive and just let you talk. If a person isn't available, you may find writing in a journal can provide support. You need to remember this exercise has an ending. There is no point in just venting non-stop. A good rule of thumb is once you start repeating yourself; it's time to move on.

Look at your options. Brainstorm ideas for alternative solutions to whatever is causing the frustration. Make a list of the things within your control. Focus on what you can do and let go of what you can't. Knowing you have options will help you feel you are not trapped.

Beware of procrastination. It is easy to avoid and put off anything that is too hard or not going anywhere. Don't delay. Keep taking steps forward. As Thomas Edison said, "Many of life's failures are people who did not realize how close they were to success when they gave up."

There are plenty of times in our life when we will feel frustrated. There's no way to avoid it. Use these struggles to come up with solutions that can help reduce your stress.

Think about this the next time you are in a line or sitting in traffic. Look for ways to occupy your mind. Play a game with yourself and see how creative you can be in using your time more productively.

FIND YOUR PASSION

Have you ever been around people who give the impression to have a perfect life? You can't imagine them being any way other than how they appear. They seem so happy, content, confident, and knowledgeable. They are having fun. You may even feel a little jealous and wish you were like them. They are passionate about whatever they are doing. You can hear it in their voices and see it in their eyes. They just seem to love what they do. I saw that the first time I met my husband and heard his story. I wanted to be a part of that enthusiasm, spirit, and energy.

Perhaps you wish you had that excitement, but feel burnt-out and no longer enjoy what you do. Are you thinking of changing your career or your life? We don't always believe we have a choice in what we do. I believe happiness and passion work together. One feeds the other.

Are you wanting to start something new in your life? How do you decide? First, look at what makes you light up when thinking about the opportunities you may have. Efforts that come easy for us are the things we enjoy and make us happy. We are most often happiest when we feel accomplishment. We enjoy feeling creative or productive.

Being knowledgeable about a subject or getting enjoyment from learning more may be a good place to start. Ask your friends and associates what they think you enjoy and what makes you get excited when engaged in conversation. You may be surprised by their answers. Many people have left well-paying careers to work in another because of their passion. That desire can bring out talent and lead to success. People with passion don't look at failure, only success.

What if you have loss your passion? Today's pressure and stress can take a toll on anyone. Have you lost your motivation? Are you looking forward to each day? Perhaps you are just showing up and going through the motions.

Most of us cannot begin a new career or start over in life. So how do you put passion back into your life? You work at it until it becomes a part of you. Your attitude will be the driving force. You have the power to be innovative and self-driven. Look for ways to enjoy what you do and make every day a little better. Be accountable to yourself. Put energy into the day and be proud of your accomplishments.

Look at what you do well and write it down. Frequently we only see the unhappy parts of life and skip over what is working well. We put too much effort focusing on the negative. We forget that our thoughts can become our reality. We repeat those stories, and reinforce them until we are soon living them. Know that the stories you are playing out in your mind can be harmful if they are negative. One of the best gifts you can give yourself is to recognize this and change your thoughts. Be aware of "mind chatter" and change your thoughts, directing them to more positive outcomes. Remember, we are never as incompetent or as insecure as our minds would like us believe. Practice being observant to what you are telling yourself.

Life is short. Don't waste your life waiting for the weekends. In the words of author H. Jackson Browne, *"Find a job you like and you add five days to every week."*

PLAY WELL WITH OTHERS

I have been fortunate enough to work with a variety of people from different walks of life. I have worked in a donut shop, a sewing factory, small mom and pop stores to large corporations. This includes working overseas in a country where I didn't speak the native language. One of the best lessons I learned from these different experiences is we all have opinions on what is correct or rude behavior. I worked with a gentleman in the Middle East who found me rude because I would say *Bye* rather than say *Goodbye* - such a small thing to me but so wrong to him.

We all find people that rub us the wrong way. They are often the personalities that don't play well with others. They often have a bad attitude. You know who they are. They are the people in the office that don't understand teamwork. They want all the glory, talk behind people's backs, spread rumors, try to make others look bad, and are sometimes dishonest.

What are the options when dealing with this kind of person? First let's start by looking at ourselves. I have some guidelines that you may want to adopt. It's not difficult to do but a good place to start. You may find these helpful so you can adjust how you deal with the difficult people in your life.

One of the best strategies is to know it's not about you. You alone have control of your behavior so pay attention to your reactions. Remember other people are projecting their reality so don't take it personally. Be the role model of how you would like to be treated.

When dealing with an uncomfortable situation you may need more information. Ask questions and work towards the best communication possible. If questions are not possible, then express what is needed, so you are understood. Many time this will clear up misunderstandings.

Another possibility for help with difficult people is to talk with a trusted friend or colleague. Brainstorm ways to address the situation. Or perhaps have a private discussion with the person you feel is difficult to work with to see if you can find common ground. When using this approach be sure to use "I feel" messages rather than attacking them with "you" messages. Stay rational when confronting a difficult person. Resist the urge to fight to win the argument.

When you actively listen and ask questions, it can help develop better relationships and sometimes even friendships.

Keep these ideas in your thoughts as it may help reduce the stress when dealing with people who you feel are difficult. You don't want to waste energy trying to change or control someone. A better strategy is to use that energy to help yourself and live a better life.

FIND YOUR MOTIVATION

Are you in a slump? Is life getting a little too hard? Feel out of control? In this nonstop world, it's easy to lose our way. We get lost and feel uninspired. It happens to everyone at some point. You have a goal and just can't find the motivation to follow through. How many times have you said, "I am going to..." and even have a plan, but somehow everyday life gets in the way? You discover it's hard to find the discipline. Whatever the reason, you lose focus.

Often these setbacks or delays happen because we have too many things going on at the same time. I find myself wanting to do everything and all at once. Being pulled in too many directions will distract us from what we intended to accomplish. It's important to know when to pull back and refocus on what is most important now. Target and accomplish one item at a time then move forward. If you have good aim on what you want, you will feel good about yourself as you achieve these tasks. That sense of accomplishment will make it easier to work on the next one. Remember how important your life and time is to you. It is up to you to use it and live each day to its fullest.

Are you a dreamer or a doer? My personality is more of a doer. If I have a dream, I work toward it rather than wishing for it. I like thinking of a dream as motivation to reach a goal. Develop a slogan or mantra you can repeat to yourself to keep that thought or goal in your head.

When I was climbing Kilimanjaro, my guide told me a mantra to repeat to myself because I was worried I would fall. He said to keep saying, *"trust your boots."* I went up that mountain saying my mantra over and over in my head and believe it or not, it helped. My purpose was to get to the top of that mountain and I had trained hard to do so but, in reality, I was afraid. The mantra helped me reinforce my goal to reach the top and get back down.

"We are what we repeatedly do. Excellence then, is not an act, but a habit" - Aristotle

"Get out and do something. Move. Interact. Explore. Breathe. Take a chance. Stop voluntarily wasting your life. Stop complaining and saying you're bored. It's your life. Do something with it. You are what you repeatedly do." - Unknown

GOOD AS YOUR WORD

Do you make promises you don't keep? Do you back out of events, occasions and appointments because you are too busy or don't feel like attending? Perhaps something comes up at the last minute and you say to yourself, *"they will understand."* Do you contact people when you say you will? Are you sincere when saying, *"let's get together soon?"* Do your friends or coworkers tease you about being unreliable, or don't believe you when you tell them you will do something? Is your word just a bunch of words?

If these questions sound familiar, then maybe you should think about the definition of dependable.

> de·pend·a·ble   [dih-pen-duh-buhl]
> -adjective - *capable of being depended on; worthy of trust; reliable.*
> -synonyms - *trustworthy, trusted, steadfast, faithful, responsible.*

Don't you hate it when someone lets you down? I am so disappointed when someone tells me they will do something and then, for whatever reason, doesn't. I am as guilty as anyone. I sometime over-obligate myself. I want to do it all. I work and play hard, but many times I can't get it all done. Sometimes, I will cancel going to an evening event because I am just too tired. Or I may call my gym partner up and cancel our workout. You know the drill. We get overwhelmed and exhausted from work, family, schedules, and the last-minute changes that happen in our lives. That brings me back to being dependable. How do we find that place where people know they can count on us and trust we are reliable and responsible?

First, I would advise to not over commit yourself. I know you want to do it and it will make someone unhappy if you say no. It will also make them unhappy if you say yes, then not show up or keep your word.

Become dependable to yourself. Do whatever it takes to get organized. Maybe start with a calendar. Work in extra time for delays, problems, or changes. You can't make commitments if you don't know what you have obligated yourself to each day. Remember, you can say *no* and people will understand. It is better to say no upfront rather than disappoint later.

Stop making excuses. It is so easy to find excuses and to blame others or circumstances. Be responsible and take control. Don't lead others to the conclusion you are not accountable. We all have choices to make every day. Be reliable, faithful, responsible.

"Be the change you want to see in the world." - Mahatma Gandhi

MIND YOUR OWN BUSINESS

Here is something you may have noticed and are hopefully avoiding. I am talking about getting into another person's business. I see this all the time - people watching each other to see what others are doing and interjecting themselves.

We can learn a lot from watching each other. Sadly, I find many are not watching to learn to grow as a person or become better in life. This behavior can create problems.

One example is getting involved in areas you should not. You may have good intentions but more than likely your comments and advice are unwanted. Another problem with obsessing on what others are doing is not taking care of your own business. Sometimes we are so busy emulating others we lose our originality. Do you want to be a follower or leader?

I have worked for companies that were so occupied with the competition they forget their own business. Instead of doing things that make them better, they try to go after what other people have (including customers and vendors) and make decisions that do not make them better businesses.

Many of you may understand this thought. You wouldn't intentionally go to a party wearing the same outfit as someone else. Are you taking care of yourself or are you being led by others?

I have watched business owners work with unique ideas, and then I see competitors copy and follow. A good example is to think of professional sports. No one cares who came in second. Like a stockcar race, spectators are watching the leader and that driver's tactics.

The following are a few ideas that distinguish a leader from a follower.

Look for weak spots in yourself or your company. Recognize them and be proactive to work on a plan of action to address them.

A leader is not always popular so prepare yourself.

When you attract people suited to you and your business you will do your best work. This creates happy customers, coworkers, vendors, and friends.

Learn how to handle positive and negative feedback. Don't take it personally and learn how you can improve. It could be the key to your next business opportunity.

Learn to delegate. Express what you need and your expectations by being specific, but leave room for people to bring their own energy to the table.

Get out of your comfort zone. You can grow in more exciting directions when you have the courage to go outside your daily box.

"That is what leadership is all about: staking your ground ahead of where opinion is and convincing people, not simply following the popular opinion of the moment." - Doris Kearns Goodwin

I WISH

How many times a day do you say, "**I wish?**" It may be for something temporary. Good examples are love, money, fame, or other things you would like to have more of in your life. You may say something of that nature often, but do nothing about it. It's just a wish. I believe we all do this, but I found some people say, "*I wish*," and dream while others say, "*I wish*," then plan to make their desires come true.

I am talking about life changes. Making changes that are so incredible you marvel how they happened. You need to want something badly to make these kinds of changes. People do it all the time, but most of us don't notice them unless we are directly involved. Over my lifetime, I occasionally run into someone who shows me what can be done when desire generates a personal journey.

Let me give you some examples:

A lady goes on a health plan and becomes a completely new person.

The business guy loses everything and wins it all back from hard work and dedication.

A man loses his sight then climbs the highest peaks in the world. The disabled woman accomplishes more than a fully functional person.

A person who faces their worst fear and teaches others how to overcome the same.

These are the people who want something so much they are willing to change everything to obtain that miracle. They believe. They believe in themselves and trust they can make the changes needed towards a better life. They have faith to follow their desires that will affect the rest of their lives.

So, the next time you say "*I wish*," think if it's enough to make the wish then plan to change.

MAKING A GAME PLAN

I have been thinking about goals - personal and business. I must confess that sometimes when people talk about setting goals, I laugh to myself. I laugh because so often it becomes just talk, and that's it. Why, you ask? I think it's because we get so occupied we find it hard to pursue what we want while taking care of everything else. We get distracted. Our priorities get out of balance. We fail to plan for our greatest needs.

But think about this - we plan our days, our meals, parties, and vacations. But we fail to plan our future and relationships. How many of us talk about losing weight, exercising, spending more time with family or friends? Plus, how much planning are you doing with your career, business or adventures? Perhaps you would like to volunteer and give back to the community. This is above and beyond taking care of your home, health, children, entertainment, finances and so on. It can be overwhelming.

We need balance. Yes, vacations are important, but we also need to have a long-term plan or direction in life.

This got me thinking about the things I want to accomplish. There are many things I want to do in my life, both personal and business. Many times I get overwhelmed and discouraged from the different directions I want to go. At the end of the year, I find I haven't accomplished as much as I had hoped.

I decided I needed to make a game plan, but a plan for the long-term. First, I wrote down what I wanted to do. Each thing I wrote on my list had to be tangible. It also had to be valuable, achievable, flexible and have a deadline.

Plus, I wouldn't write it down until I committed to the work needed. Because of the criteria, the list is short. With so much going on in my life, I don't want to add more to it. If I commit to too much, nothing will happen.

Why make a game plan? It helps you have direction. It gives you a purpose. Plus, think about the time it will save. You will know where you are going.

Someone once told me how to handle daily paperwork. Their advice was to only touch it once.

Think about this and see if you do the same. You have a box with all kinds of mail in it such as invoices, letters, etc. You look through it every day and half goes back into the box. So instead of shuffling the same papers over and over why not deal with each one and move on? File it, pay it, answer it or throw it away.

If it can't be handled right away, use a calendar file. Put it in the date you can address it and then complete the task.

Planning a direction in life will help you make decisions. It will increase your self-confidence as things get accomplished. It will help save you time.

If you are looking for help with your finances, relationships, life purpose, vocation, or your (physical, emotional, and spiritual) health, you need to start with a plan.

"Plan for the future because that's where you are going to spend the rest of your life." – Mark Twain

THE AIR AROUND YOU

I want to talk about the negative people in our lives and how to be a more positive person. Do you know people who are like a dark cloud? For example, I know people who live in constant drama. Every conversation moves immediately to all the negative things in life. Everything about them oozes negative thoughts, words, looks, and it shows even in their posture. If you're not careful, they can draw you into their world of negative messages.

How can you manage with these individuals? First, know their negativity has nothing to do with you, but it is their way of being heard. They may be unhappy with their life. They also may feel power by hurting others with their attitude.

I am sure you have been around people who like to generate a crisis just to see what reactions they can create. Remember to guard your feelings and stay out of their drama. Their negative behavior reflects their attitude and you have the control how you deal with it. Say something positive.

There is someone in my life who likes drama, so I began a habit years ago of saying something positive every time they said something negative. It did not change their behavior, but it helped me. After a while it became a game to see what I could say in response to their negative words. Then it became a habit for life. I got so much practice I would automatically answer with a positive statement. This exercise made me feel even more positive!

Don't avoid negative people in your life, but learn how to manage them. You have the control, so don't allow them to affect your feeling and thoughts. You have the power to keep your thoughts on track for you.

"Watch your thoughts; they become words. Watch your words; they become actions. Watch your actions; they become habit. Watch your habits; they become character. Watch your character; it becomes your destiny." – *Lao Tzu*

CLEANING OUT THE COBWEBS

I find people will start a little spring cleaning when the weather changes. It's when I get the urge to remove the house clutter - toss files, clear out old clothes, clean the dust out of the corners and trash the collection of magazines gathered in a pile. It's time to air out the house and start fresh again.

While talking about clutter, have you thought about clearing out your mind? A little spring cleaning inside your head? Or as I like to put it, "cleaning out the cobwebs." After all, your mind is your home for everything in life.

I was recently trying meditation - again. It's a difficult process for me to sit quietly and clear out any thoughts for meditation. I will set the stage, relax, find a quiet place and get comfortable. The problem is my mind just doesn't want to cooperate. It's thinking of all the things I should be doing.

While you may not be into yoga or meditation, you may see the benefits of clearing out the cobwebs in your life. For example, we need to dump the things that aren't working for us while adding new things into our lives that will help us.

Think about forgiving yourself and others. By choosing to forgive, you can move forward and on to better things. Think how much energy is wasted on anger, resentment, or revenge. Or maybe you need to ask for forgiveness. If so, just bite the bullet and do it. Stop worrying because it's so much better to use your mind for more positive things.

Do you ever feel like you are doing a lot of work but not accomplishing much? Maybe you need to organize all the tasks you are trying to accomplish. Make a mental list of what is important and stick with those items. Discard the ones that aren't needed or at least put them at the end of your list. Just because you have always been doing something doesn't mean you need to continue.

Give yourself a break. Have fun and put effort into a project or hobby that you love. I find I am most relaxed when I am enjoying a good book, painting, or cooking. When you are engaged with your thoughts, your actions show a different attitude. Take time to clean your mental home and feel better about yourself.

"Never again clutter your days or nights with so many menial and unimportant things that you have no time to accept a real challenge when it comes along. This applies to play as well as work. A day merely survived is no cause for celebration. You are not here to fritter away your precious hours when you have the ability to accomplish so much by making a slight change in your routine. No more busy work. No more hiding from success. Leave time, leave space, to grow. Now. Now! Not tomorrow!" - Og Mandino

MAGIC WORDS

Have you noticed people are forgetting what they were taught as children? I attended an event with an area set aside for those who paid an upgraded price to attend. A person not part of that group walked in and helped herself to the refreshments. When approached, she had an attitude of entitlement and rudeness. This started me thinking about people and their manners.

Good manners show consideration for others. Our society has become causal, and that has good and bad points. It is nice not to do some of the things that were expected years ago, but somewhere we lost what I think is important everyday respect for those around us.

Let me first start by giving you a few good manners I believe are important:

Saying please and thank you. Never intentionally embarrassing another. Not talking only about yourself. Respecting other people's space and property. Not gossiping, prying, or asking personal, intrusive questions. Not staring or pointing at someone. Dressing appropriately for the occasion. Not using your cell phone when engaged in conversation or at a meeting.

A good rule to follow is treat others like you would like to be treated. Those little things make a big difference in how you are perceived.

Bad manners can hold you back in life. You may march to your own drummer and that is okay, but when it comes to succeeding in life, manners are important. Your business dealings will be harder if clients find you awkward, distasteful or rude. A lack of basic manners is a major handicap in professional life.

Think consideration. Isn't is much nicer to have someone be helpful when doing business with them? Don't you prefer being around others that are well behaved and are respectful?

We easily forget how actions can affect others. Take a moment to think about saying *please and thank you* and I think you will find others will reciprocate.

 You can get through life with bad manners, but it's easier with good manners. - Lillian Gish

GET IT DONE

Do you remember the army commercial that told us how much they get done before nine o'clock in the morning? I have been reading about busy people. Do you feel you are always going but get little done? Are you the hamster on the wheel?

I used to work with a woman who spent the entire day going from office to cubical getting all the staff gossip without gaining work-related information. Then just as others were getting ready to leave, she would panic. Next thing you know, she would tell everyone how much work she has, how busy she is, and how long it will take her to complete her job.

We all have different priorities on goals, needs, and ways we accomplish our work. How do you get everything done for work and family, plus enjoy life as well? I have been asking myself those same questions and here are a few ideas to help you increase your daily accomplishments.

Remember that your time is important. It's important to you and to others.

Do you know where you spend your time? Like anything else, you need to know where you are before you can plan where you are going. Take the time to track how you are spending your time. It's not a fun exercise, but it will help you analyze where you can make changes for better use of your time.

A good place to start is tracking how much you are watching television. Can you record a program to watch it another time when you are not needed for other things?

Look at your workplace. Instead of spending that first fifteen minutes with coworkers talking about the previous evening, use it to get emails or other things out of the way.

Once you know where you are spending your time, then you can plan. You can decide where to spend it going forward in your personal and professional life.

Remember you are not trying to add more to your current schedule. You are making better use of your time.

Build new habits. Maybe you want to have more time in the morning to read something inspirational or take a walk before work. To do that, you may need to go to bed a little earlier.

Don't change too much too fast. Go slowly and build good habits over time.

Another idea to help make your life more balanced is to get more done in less time. Set specific goals and make a "to-do-list." But you must be accountable. Review and check your progress.

Think of a road map getting from point A to point B. Don't let distractions get in your way. Stay focus and on track.

This is about you, so set your own standards rather than following the latest fad. Find your discipline and learn to manage your time and you will have more balance in your life.

"Dost thou love life, then do not squander time, for that's the stuff life is made of." - Benjamin Franklin

TOMORROW IS ANOTHER DAY

I took a little survey on social media asking for thoughts on our biggest challenges today. The answers were all different, but also had some things in common. A few were about making time for life, family, work, and relaxation. Others were information overload, technology, health care, and crime.

This brings me to a conversation I had with a friend about being overwhelmed to the point of putting things off until later. I am talking about the subject of procrastination.

The Wikipedia definition is: "Procrastination refers to the act of replacing high-priority actions with tasks of lower priority, or doing something from which one derives enjoyment, and thus putting off important tasks to a later time."

We all procrastinate because it's natural as humans to want to do the things we enjoy over the tasks we don't. Today, we get so much information, technology, and responsibilities thrown at us, we are overwhelmed and have difficulty getting things completed.

Have you been putting something off for months? It may be something you don't want to do because it's unpleasant, or you fear what will happen. Much of procrastination comes from tasks which appear so big you can't seem to get your arms around them. If procrastination is an issue, and you want to change the circumstances, here are a few suggestions and questions you may want to ask yourself.

Recognize you are putting off the project or task. Have you developed a habit of putting things off? Ask yourself why and be honest with yourself about the answer. Is it bothering you? What are the consequences for not doing the task? Is it interfering in your life? Are the projects getting bigger and harder to complete as you continue to put them off?

There is a saying asking, *"How do you eat an elephant?"* And the answer is, *"One bite at a time."* Break projects into bites or bullet points so it does not appear to be this monster looming over you. Make a list of what needs to be done and prioritize the most important. Decide and begin to tackle each one. Learn to take pleasure in checking things off your list.

We will always have things in life we put off or don't want to do. The goal is to decide and take action.

"If you want to make an easy job seem mighty hard, just keep putting off doing it." - Olin Miller

"I can't think about that right now. If I do, I'll go crazy. I'll think about that tomorrow." - Scarlett O'Hara, Gone with the Wind

FINDING YOUR PATH

I saw the film *The Way*. As soon as I watched it, I added the five-hundred-mile El Camino de Santiago to my bucket list of things to do. To my surprise, after seeing the film a good friend emailed me she was on the trek. I believe things come to me as a sign to pay attention. The film follows a father who has a son that dies on the trail in a storm. He then goes to Spain to bring him home.

Instead of coming home, he ends up taking the pilgrimage himself and the movie revolves around him and a few of the people he meets on the trail. The father had lost the meaning of life. His son tried multiple times to point it out to his father but could not convince him. His father thought his way was the right way. Only after his son's death and walking many miles did he find the life path he needed to follow.

It almost has a *Wizard of Oz* feeling because each of the people are walking for a reason. This film reveals what we all go through in life. Everyday has its ups and downs, hardships and trials, as well as joy and happiness. We face our fears, overcome our sorrows, mistakes, and are united together with others.

The idea got me thinking about how we are all on our own path. We make decisions and find direction as part of the journey. I also thought about how easily we get lost in life.

Our society places so much emphasis on things like career, house, car, and money. I think we should be more aware of relationships, health, morals, personal value, integrity, and truth. Sometimes we don't understand what we are losing until it's too late.

The pressures of life can derail us and recovery may not happen. We must be on guard for the obstacles that stand in our way to happiness. There are many ways to reach your destination if you keep your eyes on what's important. Sometimes you must go with what is right for you against all advice.

Think of some of the greatest people in history and you will realize they followed their own path. I would recommend accepting others for who they are as they walk on their own path. Remember we have free will to create our own destiny.

"You don't choose a life, Dad...you live one."- From the movie, The Way

WHERE ARE YOU GOING

Every day we make decisions that change or touch our lives. Each decision is based on our comfort level, how it affects others, basic needs, wants and level of self-satisfaction.

Robert Frost wrote a poem about coming to a fork in the road and deciding which way to go. So often we are like cattle, herded and traveling the same direction without question. People take up a cause or do something because it is a trend. No real thought has gone into the action. I do not intend to judge these actions, but to examine the directions we take in life.

I have made decisions in my life that would be considered the road less traveled. I have also followed the path of a much-conformed life. The point is we all have a huge variety of choices. We can follow others or step outside of what is considered normal and run down the path less traveled. But how often do we take the time to think about where we are going and why?

Here are a few thoughts on why take the road less traveled.

One reason is independence. Be self-reliant. Learning the facts and making choices based on the information presented would be the road less traveled for many.

A second reason would be to focus on where you are going. Are you drifting, letting life just drag you along? Or are you thinking about where you want to be? Figure out who you are and trust yourself to know which direction to take.

Part of life is the surprises that greet us and part is the satisfaction of planning the trip while enjoying the scenery along the way. Remember you can always change directions.

You are charting your own life direction. You may find a dead end on your path or a fork in the road that leads to new and better things in life. Let yourself explore and see what the future may hold. Learning keeps us young at heart. Be bold and look for options that may open a whole new world for you.

IT'S NOT A SECRET

Several years ago, a craze swept the country that focused on a concept called the law of attraction. Its main principle is *"like attracts like."* This law is about manifesting your dreams, wants, and desires.

We can be positive, negative, happy or sad. It's our choice. If you want and desire something enough, you will find ways to get it. If you truly want to have more money, you can earn it, and if you want to lose those extra pounds you will by setting your mind to the end result.

You will have obstacles that will get in the way. And they will be difficult. We all run into road-blocks and need to find our way through or around them.

Sometimes we can be delayed for a time while dealing with a difficult part of life. You have the power to manifest the results you want. You have the tools to create the determination, purpose and goal.

Getting to the goal, dream, or the things you want and desire is not an easy task. But if you are willing to pay the toll, you will achieve the results you are working toward. Remember, you will do what you are thinking and feeling because our thoughts guide us. We create our own circumstances. We have the power within.

"The only journey is the one within." - Rainer Maria Rilke

MAKE A PLAN

Plan? What Plan? I saw a quote about how we don't plan to fail, but fail to plan. Sound familiar? Many of us don't plan, we don't have a strategy for a household budget, exercise routine, retirement, college expense, or business. Many people use what I call the knee-jerk plan. You know this plan; it's the plan of the moment or the instant gratification.

We have good intentions. We know where we want to end up but, somehow, the actual journey to get there is a little foggy. Here are a few questions I would suggest you ask yourself.

Do you know where you are going and where you want to be? What is your intended destination? Are you on a path of construction or destruction?

Maybe you are not in great health, but you keep doing the same things day in and day out hoping the results will be different.

Perhaps you allow others to influence your decisions. Do you follow others because everyone is doing it? I see business decisions made this way all the time. They are chasing the competition and following their competitors path.

Many decisions are made because we think or are told that someone else is more intelligent and successful, so we should listen and follow their path. Many companies count on that exact reaction and they structure their plans around our need to belong.

Do you have a vision of what you want to be, how you want your business to run, where you see your family in the future? Sometimes we see what we want and take little side trips along the way. I have done that many times in my career. I had a long-term goal of what I wanted in my career, but the path I took was not the traditional one. The results led me to many things others have not experienced.

I urge you to not limit yourself with strict rules. Change is okay but always keep in mind that the decisions you are making today should look at the long-term goal and not the instant gratification.

"Strategic planning is worthless - unless there is first a strategic vision." - John Naisbitt

WHAT'S IN IT FOR ME?

So much of our life is about by the acronym WIIFM. You may not know what it stands for although you either think or use it daily. Business organizations have used it over several decades to persuade or motive. And because of our society, we have become somewhat immune to putting others first and think only about - *What's In It For Me?*

For an owner in a sales or service culture, this question, when directed to customers and clients, can make a business more successful. If you can answer that question for them, they will see how your business will benefit them and that makes you a good fit. But too many people use this thought process as a way of making life decisions. If we place too much emphasis thinking only of our benefits, the hidden message is that acting in one's self-interest is acceptable. That thinking can lead to behaviors that are not always acceptable.

I would urge you to balance out your WIIFM with PIF or "Pay It Forward." You may have seen the movie of the same name or have heard the phrase. The idea to repay good deeds received by one person by doing good deeds for others.

We still have people that are selfless; who go above and beyond giving back to others, their community, and country. My hope is, as a society, we are not so absorbed in ourselves we forget to see the big picture and give back. Perhaps we can change the tide of entitlement and narcissism that seems to be more prevalent than in the past.

Instead of wondering what's in it for us, perhaps we can wonder how to reach out and pay it forward.

"I expect to pass through the world but once. Any good therefore that I can do, or any kindness I can show to any creature, let me do it now. Let me not defer it, for I shall not pass this way again." - Stephen Grellet

THE MAGIC PILL

Are you still looking for that magic pill? It's the one that will reduce wrinkles, fat, gain muscle, and solve all the daily problems like money, emotions and stress. This magic pill will be extra special because it will solve all our struggles and cure our pain. If only I could invent that magic pill!

This pill would be used for the hard stuff in life we put off and do not want to face each day. It would help with the decisions we make about taking care of ourselves and others. These are the decisions that require thought and discipline.

I am talking about the decisions that do not give us instant gratification. The magic pill will do that for us. We would no longer need to think about how our choices affect our life. All our time could be spent on doing what we want.

We wouldn't have to worry about our health or wellbeing. No problems with retirement, taxes or what is happening in the world. We would be forever young, beautiful, innocent and happy. Everyone would love us and the world would be the happiest of places. It could be a snap with the magic pill.

A word of warning:

The magic pill comes with side effects, as do most drugs.

You would lose the satisfaction of accomplishment, become bored from the day-to-day routine without challenge.

You would lose the simple pleasures in life.

There would be no need to work out, work hard, have commitments or earn anything. No new places to see because you really don't care. No drive, goals, or dreams.

Hmmm, maybe this magic pill is not the great thing I thought it would be. Perhaps it's not needed. Besides, I bet it would be too large to swallow and have a bad after taste too.

"If you actually succeed in creating a utopia, you've created a world without conflict, in which everything is perfect. And if there's no conflict, there are no stories worth telling - or reading!" - Veronica Roth

MAKING EACH DAY A GIFT

Are you living each day to the fullest? You may find it easy to put off your future. You may think about things you want to do or change in your life but put it off for a later time. Perhaps the following information will help you break out of this stagnation and make changes in your life.

Listen to your inner self. Pay attention to your feelings and what you are thinking. Understand your values and your requirements. Think about who and what inspires you and what choices can be made to help fulfill your individual needs.

Write down these thoughts to help you consolidate and confirm your needs. Once you put it on paper you can work on a plan. Where do you see yourself in a year, five years or even ten?

Establish goals from this exercise to discover who you are and what you want. Then, narrow them down to the most important. Choose the ones you can control, the ones that fit your needs best, and let go of the rest. You can add or subtract as you grow and accomplish these goals.

Take time to disconnect. Get in touch with yourself and nature. Put away technology. Work on keeping balance in your approach to life and focusing on the benefits you are aiming toward. Keep your core principles and beliefs close even when the pressure and challenges from the outside makes it hard to continue.

Establishing your values, goals and priorities will help you move toward achieving balance in life. Give yourself the gift of taking care of yourself and living your life to the fullest.

"Life is a gift to you. The way you live your life is your gift to those who come after. Make it a fantastic one." - Barb Schmit

"The best day of your life is the one on which you decide your life is your own. No apologies or excuses... The gift is yours—it is an amazing journey—and you alone are responsible for the quality of it." - Bob Moawad

SILVER LININGS

I was accused of becoming a negative person. Imagine my gasping surprise! My first thought was, "You can't be talking to me!" I don't quite remember if I said those words, but I know the thought went through my head. But the person who shared this information cares for me and I know that it was given with good intentions.

I thought about it and realized that I am the type of person who sees dark clouds in most situations. I don't know if it's from the many challenges I have faced in the past, learned behaviors, or just plain habit. I had quit looking for the silver linings in my life. I had forgotten about gratitude.

I will allow myself a little leeway as I am a practical person and look for the holes in an argument or the negative side of the plan. That aside, I sometimes forgot to look for the upside in situations. I let the dark clouds obscure the bright spots in life.

Once I realized what I was doing, I set my path to look for the good and have gratitude for the wonderful things that have come my way, past and present.

So often, we get together with family or friends and conversations move to the negative side of life. We complain about our job, children, money, or neighbors. It's a habit to complain and look at the negative side of things.

You can change the tide of negative thoughts or words by writing. Start a journal and add positive statements to your conversations. Look for the good in your life. Thank your family and friends for the wonderful things they add to your life.

I have been shown what others do out of kindness and I have been speechless with gratitude. Giving thanks is a great reminder of the good in so many things.

When you are feeling the dark clouds around you, ask yourself what you can learn from this situation. What is the lesson or purpose that will help or answer something from your past?

Does this situation have an opportunity that can help you or someone else? Does this open new thoughts or ways of doing things?

Find a mantra to help keep your thoughts positive. There are many thoughts you can find for your mantra, but I will leave you with this as an example.

"Be Thankful Be thankful that you don't already have everything you desire. If you did, what would there be to look forward to? Be thankful when you don't know something, for it gives you the opportunity to learn.

Be thankful for the difficult times. During those times you grow. Be thankful for your limitations because they give you opportunities for improvement. Be thankful for each new challenge because it will build your strength and character.

Be thankful for your mistakes, they will teach you valuable lessons.

Be thankful when you're tired and weary because it means you've made a difference. It is easy to be thankful for the good things. A life of rich fulfillment comes to those who are also thankful for the setbacks.

GRATITUDE can turn a negative into a positive. Find a way to be thankful for your troubles and they can become your blessings."- Unknown

DAY TO DAY

A good friend shared her pastor's sermon and how it rang true to her life. The sermon was about living life or surviving day to day. Like her, the subject had my attention. I have been thinking about that conversation ever since, looking at my life and what I have been doing.

If asked, I believe most of us would answer the question as *living* rather than *surviving*. But if you look deeply enough, I believe the answer may change. If you ask someone "How are you doing?" Often the responses are, "Hanging in there." Or "Surviving."

You may be surprised if you look up the definition of living. Here are some of the things I found: *having life, active, functioning, and exhibiting the life or motion of nature, full of life or vigor, true to life.*

Some synonyms were *alive, live, having life, animate.*

The meaning of surviving is quite the opposite. I found these: *continue to live, remain or continue in existence, to get along unaffected despite some occurrence, endure or live through, continue to exist in spite of danger or hardship, persevere, exist.*

Synonyms are - *remain alive, live, sustain oneself, pull through, get through, hold on/out, make it, keep body and soul together.*

I began to see a fine line between the two words. Often survival is based on a fear - fear of something or someone, fear of debt, emotions, and change. If you are just "surviving" you are pretty much sleepwalking through your life. There are triggers that warn me I am in a surviving mode. My thoughts will be, *When I get through this…. Or when this happens I can do that…* I have learned to recognize this is a pattern.

There will always be obstacles in life. How you react, plan and move forward is where the difference between living and surviving takes place.

Often our world makes us believe all the negative things that happen to us are life threatening. Much of it is from the stress of overindulging. We forget our own self-worth.

The following are a few thoughts on living life.

Start by developing your focus. Society is teaching us to adapt to a shorter attention span. Focus on the important things in life that help you and those who are important to you.

Work on simplifying your life. Make conscious decisions on the things you need in life and not the latest trend.

Find your peace. None of us are perfect but we can find inner peace.

Seek out the things that give you interest and deep satisfaction.

Create choices for living life. That may mean a focus on your work, relationship, career or finances. All these areas can put you under the survival threat, so look at getting rid of the burdens, and find the balance in your life.

"When life was worrying about a car payment or a rent payment and a bill, you're so consumed with that, you really don't have time to know yourself. That's surviving and getting by." - Fred Durst

"Make treating yourself a priority and always remember your life is happening now. Don't put off all your dreams and pleasures to another day. In any balanced personal definition of success there has to be a powerful element of living life in the present." - Mireille Guiliano

DUMP THE CLUTTER

Have you noticed how people have more than they need? I'm sure you have seen the yard, garage, and community sales. Out with the old and make room for the new. Right? Have you thought about removing the clutter in your life?

How many things are you carrying around in life that muddles your mind and affects your health? Is it time to deal with emotions or to make behavioral changes to be a healthier person? Getting the clutter out of your head is a little harder to manage than going through the closet. It may take a little more effort, but the principles are the same.

In a closet, you throw out the items that are old, out of style, no longer fit or were a mistake buy. Another example is stored items in your garage. It's just there in case you may need it, or it's still in working condition so you may use it again.

Now put that into perspective for your life. Are you carrying around emotions that are no longer valid? If so, find out why you are feeling the emotion and if you need to forgive yourself and make peace with the cause. Maybe you have a habit of being the victim of circumstance. If so, maybe it's time to look at what is happening, what you can control, and identify who to stop blaming for those circumstances.

Do you need to evaluate the people in your life? Are they or you causing a toxic connection? Sometimes releasing the toxic energy in your relationships will change the stress in your life.

Are you a control freak who needs everything done your way? Isn't it funny how that works? You are the person who ends up doing everything because others cannot do it right. Give up that control and let others do something for you. It may not be how you would do it but think of the freedom you will gain. Often, you will gain more than what you believe you are losing.

The point is to think about the people and things in your life. You can create new and better habits that will bring improved results to your future.

Think about how you feel once the closet, garage, or whatever you are cleaning out is completed. You have a feeling of accomplishment. Clean out your life and you will find space for new ideas and other thoughts you did not have room for previously.

"What lies behind you and what lies in front of you, pales in comparison to what lies inside of you." - Ralph Waldo Emerson

THE JUDGE

Every month, I have something going on that gives me an idea for writing, speaking or a conversation with others. Some months, I feel very inspired. Other times, I find it difficult to come up with the right words.

Sometimes I write about what I have seen in others and hope it brings value to another.

For now I want to talk about judging others.

Is it possible not to be judgmental? I don't think so, and sometimes a judgment can save you from being hurt or disappointed.

On the flip side, I caution you to withhold judgment until you have been respectful enough to find out a few things.

Judging others is almost a national pastime. We see and hear it though media, politicians, coworkers, family and friends. All judging and criticizing people.

Judging others is something we do naturally. Some of the ways we judge are based on religion, appearance, disability, beliefs, jobs, race, as well as financial and community status. Often our judgments are based on a measurement to our own lives and beliefs.

We may form these decisions for a variety of reasons we don't associate with judging others. It's just an opinion. More than likely, we formed an opinion because of something that happened whether it was directed at us or someone else.

Most often, we don't know the person we are judging. We don't understand their situation. Plus, we have unrealistic expectations of people. This is the judging I am focusing on here. Ask yourself why you are judging. Are you only looking at the superficial elements, or criticizing out of habit? How would you feel if you were being judged?

Judgment should not be based on just feelings and first impressions. I am sure we miss many good connections because of our critical opinions that close off opportunities for new friendships, education, and personal fulfillment. I urge you to judge carefully and cautiously.

"Everything we hear is an opinion, not a fact. Everything we see is a perspective, not the truth." - Marcus Aurelius

SALTY NOSE

I was fortunate enough to go to the beach for an overnight trip. My room was overlooking the beach with an outside balcony. The crashing waves always have a soothing effect on me and gives the chant of *calm down, slow down.*

The next morning, sitting on the balcony, having my first cup of coffee, I noticed a group of people gathering on the beach to watch the sunrise. As the sun came up, and the sky caught fire with a multitude of colors, a few dolphin appeared and gave everyone a thrill. Pelicans began an aerodynamic show while the sun rose and the morning became alive and active as a new day started.

While sitting there enjoying the moment I thought of the saying, *"stop and smell the roses "*or, in this case, what I call a *"salty nose"* minute. I suppose the group on the beach were on vacation and their sunrise was as special as it gets for many. I wondered if they have those special moments at home. Do they stop to look at the sunrises, spend special times with their friends and family regularly?

Having an appreciation and gratitude for the relationships and blessings in our lives helps us to have more satisfaction, according to a Rutgers University study. The study suggested when people take time to appreciate the good things in life, they are happier.

Remembering special dates and celebrating time with your family, parents, children and friends are memories you and others will cherish. Find time to share yourself, listen to others and be there with them at that moment.

To appreciate life and the wonderful things around us, we need to take the time to notice. So, my thought for you to take away is to once a day stop for a few moments and either enjoy the world around you or share a moment or conversation with someone and give yourself a cherished memory.

Whenever you think you don't have the time or want to expend the effort remember that the roses are temporary, soon they will be gone, and you cannot experience that moment again.

"Yesterday's the past, tomorrow's the future, but today is a gift. That's why it's called the present." - Bil Keane

THE POWER OF WORDS

I received a compliment, and it filled me with pride and a sense of self-worth. Expressed words have so much power. Words convey pain, love, joy, compassion, peace, anger, and understanding just to name a few.

Words are powerful. They can evoke a level of joy and happiness or a depth of sadness and despair. Words said to and about others are the most powerful. What you say is received in different ways and negative words can be damaging. Our words reflect what we think too. I read a line that said, "Language is the expression of thought. Every time you speak, your mind is on parade." What does your parade say about you? Are you building others up or tearing them down with your words? Our words can either attract others or repel them. We have the choice of how and when to use them.

Words also can reflect our attitudes about a situation. Tony Robbins has said our vocabulary can change our lives and destiny by choosing the words we use to describe our emotional state. For example, if you are in the habit of saying you are **furious**, but instead say you are **irritated**, the feeling attached to those words are different and reflect a different experience accurate or not. It's the thought in your mind. Same goes for being asked how you feel, and you reply **okay** or **wonderful**! The words we say becomes our experience.

Dale Carnegie's first principle is "Don't criticize, condemn, or complain." And as hard as that may be to follow I would give you his thoughts and moral from a story within his book, *How to Win Friends and Influence People*. Carnegie's story, "Father Forgets" and the moral is:

> *Instead of condemning people, let's try to understand them. Let's try to figure out why they do what they do. That's a lot more profitable and intriguing than criticism; and it breeds sympathy, tolerance, and kindness. "To know all is to forgive all."*

Good life lesson and food for thought. You have so much power with your words. Use them wisely.

"You need to be aware of what others are doing, applaud their efforts, acknowledge their successes, and encourage them in their pursuits. When we all help one another, everybody wins." - Jim Stovall

MAKING CONNECTIONS

The end of September brings the end of summer and signs begin to show little changes in the morning air. Our days begin to get shorter.

This is the time of the year I long for cooler weather and am thankful when I can travel to the mountains. The trip gives me the chance to get an early start on the fall season with the fresh air and morning chill. A week-long car trip is always full of adventures, new discoveries and connections.

I feel most fortunate because I have a wealth of good connections in my life. These connections are important. As we move more into a digital world, we can lose some of our connective feelings to others.

Psychology studies have shown that having connections is one of the most important things in life. The influences in your life may be your spouse, relatives, close friends, mentors, teachers, or coaches. These strong ties are vital as they provide a network and closeness with others.

Good relationships with just a few people can improve our health, happiness and well-being. We have a feeling of support and emotional strength.

Research has shown that people with good relationships and friendships are, overall, happier and more satisfied with their lives. They also are more energetic, have better mental health and sometimes, live longer.

Characteristics of close relationships are the ability to love and be loved, have mutual understanding and care for another. Those associations also create a feeling of self-worth, security and help influence us to grow and learn.

Look at your relationships in life and see if you need to work your circle of family and friends. If so, here are a few tips to help you get started.

Give positive appreciative comments. You would think this happens without thought, but telling others you love them, are thankful, or congratulate and praise them will bring healthier relationships.

Also make time for them. Meet them for lunch or do an activity together. And if you have a disagreement, you need to have a non-drama, fair, calm, attentive discussion. But even more important; you may not agree, but need to move on without grudges.

Build connections in life to increase a happier and healthier existence. Focus on the good things in people while remembering we are not always perfect.

Don't miss opportunities to enjoy others. Give yourself the gift of close relationships.

"Just as the wave cannot exist for itself, but is ever a part of the heaving surface of the ocean, so must I never live my life for itself, but always in the experience which is going on around me." — Albert Schweitzer

TAKE THE STEP

We are all waiting for something most of the time. It's just a part of living. As I grow older, my patience is often short, but I have learned having patience can be a good thing. For example, one evening, heading home on the boat, I looked up, and the stars were so bright and clear, I felt I could reach out and touch them.

I wanted to get home because the day had been long, and it was the end of a weekend with Monday responsibilities ahead. On the other hand, I wanted to just sit out on the water and stare at the night sky in all its beauty.

So often our waiting involves a lot of wishing. *I wish* is an easy start to a sentence that can lead to a dead-end involving procrastination. I have studied the subject of initiative and not waiting for permission to either contribute or to act. There are individuals who fear to begin new things or to take risks and in doing so, they end up not fulfilling their potential. The point of this thought process is to do it now and don't wait. Sometimes that can be a little uncomfortable. To just do something without planning could send you off in too many directions at once. I believe we need to understand that nothing happens until we take the first step. That leap can lead to many roads. But until that first step, you cannot see change or accomplishment.

I am sure you have heard the saying, "I'm waiting for my ship to come in." This saying may have some believe the process of waiting will bring you whatever you want. You may be waiting for fame, fortune or contentment. Waiting for the situation to be perfect will not move you towards your dream or goal. Don't look for others' approval, either. The stars may never line up to the perfect formation to lead you on your path. It very well may be that you start and fail and then you start again but, with each experience, you will learn something to continue.

Remember to set aside some time to look back and note what you did over the last twelve months. What were the good things? Did you put something off that you can start now? What do you want to accomplish tomorrow and where do you want to be this time next year? Are you wishing and waiting for that ship to come in? Or will you be building your dreams even if it may be a little uncomfortable starting today?

"A journey of a thousand miles begins with a single step." - Lao-tzu

IT'S A DOG'S WORLD

I have observations about dogs that I would like to share in relation to our work, social and personal experiences.

Perhaps you have heard the term "Alpha Dog." Alphas are generally dominant in nature, but not necessarily. We may think of an alpha dog as a big bully type of dog but it's far from the truth.

I have found that a small, cute animal can be an alpha. It commands the room, announcing he or she is in charge and people need to pay attention. Alphas ignore the fact they may be small and could be crush by a larger species. They demand attention, respect and want you to know they are in control.

I am sure you know many people in your life that are alpha personalities. They are leaders, take-charge people, and confident in their decisions.

Although there are many mixes and degrees of alpha personalities, they tend to be strong, dominant, and leaders. They are composed, driven and passionate.

Another dog personality trait is the "Omega Dog." This is the exact opposite of the alpha. I see this with the dog that has begun life without good structure or guidance from the start. They are timid, shy, afraid and cower. The other dogs may bully them or ignore them completely. In the pack ranking, they are looked as the weakest link. This dog is a happy follower to an alpha.

I have met people that are the same. Omega personalities have terms used to describe them as awkward, uninspiring, bizarre interests, and eccentric. They are loners, isolated, and lack social skills. Because they are often bullied, they may lash out in defense. Society often discards the omega personalities.

The "Beta Dog" is the second in command. It will take charge if given the opportunity. The "Beta Dog" has confidence, but less than the alpha and much more than the omega. They are social, wanting to please and can be dominant, but not a leader. Beta's want to be in charge, but may not have the skills to be a true leader.

Beta people are similar. They are a mix of pleasing others, avoiding conflict and seeking approval. Betas want to solve problems. They have confidence but don't have to prove their value, especially in materialistic terms. They work well with others and collaborate rather than challenge.

We are more alike than different. People, like dogs, have their personalities with good and bad days.

For humans, it is helpful to recognize the people around us and know their traits. We have a mixture of all the behaviors and some are stronger than others.

Think about your own personality traits and where your tendencies lie. It may help you get along in the world a little better.

"Dogs don't rationalize. They don't hold anything against a person. They don't see the outside of a human but the inside of a human."—Cesar Millan

PATIENCE – PLEASE!

I am forever being tested for my patience and that has never been one of my best features. I always want quick, sudden results. Whatever the case, I want results now!

Often, I must dig deep to find patience with myself for projects I am working on or goals I want to achieve. I will beat myself up for not reaching whatever I wanted within a certain time frame. But, I also need tolerance with the multitude of small (often annoying) things that happen daily.

Over a lifetime, I have accomplished grand things when I am patient. I have found that good things come if I can wait or tolerate delays. It has helped me to climb mountains, run great distances, achieve career heights and enjoy many wonderful personal moments. The flip side (when I am not patient) is frustration, irritation, missed opportunities, and stress.

Is patience a virtue? I believe it is, and it's a lesson worth learning. In our instant gratification world today, the courage and resilience to wait is almost nonexistent. The lack of tolerance or being impatient because someone is slow, opinionated, stubborn, or arrogant will lead to judgment and anger. This, more often or not, leads to a break down in relationships. The lesson of being understanding and charitable by showing patience is tough. Being intolerant leads to the path of judgmental, critical, selfish, and lazy.

Finding patience helps avoid making impulsive decisions. It also helps with the urges of feeling greedy and selfish. Developing patience will affect your attitude with others and may give you more joy in life as well as reduce your stress. It will give you self-control and give you a sense of calmness. Finding tolerance within yourself and in others will give you a sense of self-appreciation and to enjoy what you have right now.

It teaches we are not in control of the world and don't have to be the driving force of all that is around us. Work on your patience and see the remarkable results you will find over time.

"Patience is not simply the ability to wait - it's how we behave while we're waiting."- Joyce Meyer

CHERISHED MEMORIES

Each day we receive reminders to look forward. Looking forward to tomorrow rather than reliving yesterday is a good way to live your life. But there is something to be said for keeping your cherished memories close and using them in your day-to-day living.

I recently read a question asking about your most treasured memory. I thought for a few moments and came up with several. Some of them made me smile and others were tearful, but precious all the same.

We can and do make treasured memories daily, especially if we are watchful and aware.

Look at some of the special memories in your life. These memories may be life-changing events such as your wedding day, or the birth of a child. Perhaps you have extraordinary moments of accomplishments, or they may be as simple as sitting with a loved one sharing coffee and a sunrise. Whatever the reason, we have many moments in life that bring powerful recollections.

Most everything that happens gives us knowledge to learn and grow. Each of these experiences are not only a moment in our life to look back upon, but they can help us with our future skills.

These flashes of our life's special moments can give peaceful experiences. Every day we are creating memories that will be with us as we look back. We can find these memories to be delightful times and wonderful experiences of times gone by.

Live your best life and the wonderful experiences that surround you and your loved ones. You are creating a scrapbook of cherished remembrances that will be with you always.

"Cherish the fabulous, the fantastic, the beautiful, the graceful, the moments of abandon, laughter, quirkiness. Cherish the tiny incredible details, the gigantic and varied display, and the infinite depths of life." - Jay Woodman

DID YOU SAY NO?

If you have children, you will relate to what I will say. If you do not have children, then think about those you have seen and you will understand my point. Children are fascinating to watch when they hear the word "No." I don't think they hear the word, they just find another way to ask.

My first sales training was a mantra of "**no** *is just a step closer to a* **yes**." I also remember another saying of "if *someone tells you* **no** *it's because you have not given enough reasons to say* **yes**."

All those beliefs of persistently working to a yes are true. But the flip side is to scrutinize why you received a no and if you may need to reexamine what you are trying to accomplish. The no you are getting today may mean you need to regroup and see if you are going in the right direction.

The word no is a form of rejection. I know few people that look, or want to be rejected. Rejection has many forms and most can be very hurtful.

I have received many rejections in my life, some of which were devastating. I can still see my first crush who rejected me and how devastating that felt. It was a very painful beginning to my teenage years. He used me to make his girlfriend jealous and then dropped me like a hot potato when she wanted him back. I was shocked and hurt. At that time, I didn't realize it was a good thing for me. I did not need someone that uses others for their own gain, not caring the pain it caused. Lesson learned.

I have been rejected in my career many times and in a multitude of ways. There have been jobs I thought perfect for me, but no interview was given. Most often the result from this disappointment was a better opportunity around the corner.

Many rejections in my career were from people not wanting my product or service. I would find it incredulous that someone didn't want what I offered. I couldn't understand at the time but then a bigger picture would emerge. A better offer or bigger sale would be down the road and all rejections would fade away.

So often it's easy to tell others not to worry. You may hear things like - *another opportunity is on the way, just around the corner, waiting for the right time to emerge.*

Since I am an impatient person, I have difficulty with that type of talk, but it's true. You may find some of the following information useful to help with the hurt, disappointment, and other feelings from rejection.

Rejection can hurt. Don't beat yourself up over it. We can pick ourselves apart about all the whys, could haves, and should haves, but it will not help. Note your strong qualities and give yourself emotional support. Guy Winch, a psychologist and author, spoke at a *TED Talk* discussing how we need to give ourselves emotional health on the same level as we do with our physical health. Think about that and learn to give yourself support.

Remember that rejection can help you grow. Most often, the rejection you feel is not personal. Many services or sales rejections have nothing to do with you. In fact, the person saying no may not even know why they are turning down the opportunity. Other types of rejection may involve you but can easily be about someone else and you are not the focus.

Each time you hear a **no**, regroup, see other opportunities and perhaps find something better. Negative thoughts can only stop you from learning and growing. Don't let that happen. Find the positive so you can move onward to what you need, see and do.

"A rejection is nothing more than a necessary step in the pursuit of success." - Bo Bennett

"When you're following your inner voice, doors tend to eventually open for you, even if they mostly slam at first." - Kelly Cutrone

WHAT GOES AROUND

Newton's third law states, "For every action, there is an equal and opposite reaction."

A good example of how this works is a person using force to propel themselves in water while swimming. By using their arms to push the water backward it propels them forward. One action is causing another reaction.

So how does that work when we interact with the people around us each day? Look at the law of Karma which can be the spiritual equivalent of Newton's Law of Motion.

The philosophy is for every action an energy is created that returns to us. Another way to phase this is, "you reap what you sow." I will admit that sometimes is appears Karma is slow to return. It may take years to see how a person's actions return to them, whether good or bad.

Think about how you relate with others. Do you think of the consequences of your choices when you are working out an issue or details with another?

Here are a few examples of how those actions or reactions may go when applying this to real life.

An employer who is suspicious of his employees builds distrust and will lose good workers because of his actions.

A person who treats others with disrespect will not receive respect.

People who abuse others whether mentally or verbally create an atmosphere of negativity.

On the flip side, individuals that treat others with respect and trust will develop good relationships, gain friendships, customers and friends. It's really about how we treat one another. Often people treat others as a reflection of how they feel about themselves.

How we feel and treat all concerned reflect upon us as individuals. Ask yourself this question. What are the consequences of this choice or action and how will it affect me and others?

Even though we sometimes may want to strike back in defense or anger, think about what Buddha said, "Getting angry with another person is like throwing hot coals with bare hands; both people get burned."

Put that into perspective when thinking about others. You alone have the power. You have the choice to take the higher road and focus on what will help you live a better existence.

Remember their actions reflect how they feel about themselves and you have the choice how you respond. I would remind you to remember to think before you react and break the cycle. Frequently you will find your actions can diffuse a situation and improve a relationship.

"How people treat you is their karma; how you react is yours." - *Wayne Dyer*

DISCOVERING THE WORLD

Life is an adventure, but only if you look for it and allow it to happen. It has always surprised me when people travel and never venture outside their hotel. My thoughts always turn to *why did they leave town*? They could have done the same thing at a hotel at home. I am talking about discovery and a sense of adventure to learn and explore.

I have friends who travel and not go beyond the hotel, planned tour, or try any food outside of what they were used to having at home. I know of someone that went to Europe only to complain, "those people didn't even speak English," and to find fault because it was all foreign!

I was fortunate to experience a sense of adventure at an early age. My lessons were to be curious, enjoy what the world offers, and to seek out different environments. I find it thrilling to discover and see another way of life.

Think about the last time you went somewhere on vacation. An amusement park is a good example. These types of surroundings are full of fun and safe ways to experience a multitude of new things. You can try different food, watch people, see families from all walks of life, and attempt something you would not try otherwise. Have you ever stepped out to the edge and look over the cliff of your existence?

My mother gave me that sense of adventure. She was ready at a moment's notice to go. It was thrilling for her to see new places or experience an area that was a little forbidden. She was excited to see to the red-light district in Amsterdam so she could tell her friends. Learning to used chopsticks in Europe made her laugh. In Hawaii, although frightened because she did not swim, she boarded a catamaran. She was that way from childhood to the end of her life. She instilled that sense of adventure and curiosity in all her children and grandchildren. We all want to see what is over the next mountain, or around the next bend. Other places and people are interesting and we never let a good trip get away from us or be wasted.

One of my goals in life is to not become stale. I have always been a fan of the *Star Trek* series as it has resonated with me when they would say, "explore strange new worlds, to seek out new life... boldly go..."

I urge you to step out there and look over the world at your doorstep. See what life can offer you. Enjoy a different view. Learn how others live, work, and play. Give yourself permission to grow and soak in the knowledge from the world around you.

"A sense of adventure is not taught, but caught from those around you that are curious." - Sandra Wyant

DOING THINGS DIFFERENTLY

Many of us grew up in a world where we were told what and how we should behave. I can still hear my mother telling me, *"Because I said so!"* when I questioned her direction.

We were taught to be normal. Normal has changed a lot over the decades. As an adult, we question our direction and many times fall into the trap of what is expected or considered standard. This may be driven by what is expected from family, friends and coworkers. Also pressure comes from our social environment. We need to question why we do the things we do if we expect to have certain results.

Many of us want something different in life but just can't seem to find the right direction. What is stopping us? For some of us, it's fear. Fear of failing and the embarrassment of others knowing we failed. Or, possibly, we are waiting for approval. We need others to buy into our passion or dreams to start our journey.

If you are on the path to make changes in your life, then I would tell you to begin with your own beliefs about your impending journey. Do you believe this is the right direction for you to go?

Your beliefs and priorities are great motivators for moving into a new direction. But these beliefs and priorities must outweigh the fear you have, and they must not be dependent on the approval of others.

You will not make necessary changes or do things differently until the need is greater than the consequences. Begin by knowing this is not a perfect world. You will experience mistakes, issues and some failure. That is fine. Plan for what you can up front and look to the future with an open mind. The only way to learn and move forward is by taking steps that sometimes will be missteps.

Here is an example. I was a heavy smoker many years ago. It was a habit started when I was young. Over the years, the habit had become expensive and was making me sick. Even so, I did not want to quit. I was hooked and afraid of the pain I'd feel from the cravings if I stopped. Then one day I went on a trip to a completely different environment. I was around people that did not smoke or want to be around it. The effort to figure out how and when I could smoke a cigarette was stressful. I realized how smoking was leading me on a road to an unhealthy and poor existence. The experience opened a new world for me and I started on a fresh journey.

This catalyst began a change that led from one good experience to another. It was difficult to quit. I had to break habits that had been a part of my life for many years. But the overall fact is that I wanted to quit. I wanted to feel better. The pain of smoking was greater than not smoking. Quitting became a priority, and I did things differently based on my needs going forward in life.

Don't lose sight of what you want to do in your life. It comes down to what you believe, want, and need. Focus on what you want in the future and not what you are leaving in the past. Trust yourself to set your path to do things a little differently.

"Things do not change; we change," - Henry David Thoreau

HAVING GRATITUDE

I have a friend who wrote in a daily journal what she was grateful for over a period of thirty days. She had been going through a tough time and wanted to focus on the good in her life rather than the worry, stress, and unhappiness she had been experiencing. Once started, she made it public by posting her thoughts of gratitude on social media each day.

Now think about this for a moment. Can you name thirty things you claim gratitude for and the reasons for your feeling? I can imagine you can come up with some things at first but can you really put thought into the idea and state the reasons?

I believe many of you will say you are grateful for your faith, family, friends, pets, or career. These are wonderful features in life for appreciation. But when it comes right down to it are you truly appreciative and do you find depth to your feelings?

So often we pass through this world not realizing what we have and how fortunate we are. We have expectations and don't see how the smallest thing can bring us joy.

Do you feel passionate about your life? Do you see how much you have and do you share with others how grateful you are?

I challenge you to write each day one thing you have gratitude for and why. Do you think it could change the way you think? Or how it may affect your day? Don't misunderstand; there will still be negative things that happen in your life. But you may find expressing your thankfulness daily can help with perspective. It may assist you to see life's journey when setbacks occur. Focusing on the positive can help change your outlook on life.

The science of gratitude shows us that keeping a journal of items we are thankful for can help with our satisfaction in life. Research has shown the benefits of better sleep, stronger immune systems, and positive emotions are connected to having gratefulness in life.

The focus of being grateful can provide benefits in all areas of life; social, health, career, spiritual and emotional, leading to more happiness overall.

So how do you get started on the journey to having more gratefulness in your life? You can start small with taking notice of the world and the beauty that surrounds you.

Include acts of kindness in your daily life. It could be just a smile, kind words, helping others, or focusing on the good rather than the negative. Over time, you will find you have developed a habit.

Having gratitude is a skill you can develop and bring new and positive benefits into your life.

Take the time to look at what you have in life to appreciate; then celebrate the wonder and moments of bliss.

"Cultivate the habit of being grateful for every good thing that

comes to you, and to give thanks continuously. And because all things have contributed to your advancement, you should include all things in your gratitude." - Ralph Waldo Emerson

BEGIN ANEW

Have you given thought to how much you can do with a whole year to bring more joy and fulfillment to yourself? Beginnings have so much promise for achievements and new adventures. We can be a better person, live our days to the fullest, and really make some life changes. I'm getting pumped up just thinking about the possibilities.

But, do you have fixed thought syndrome? Are you looking at the same list of goals you did previously, knowing your resolve will last only a few days, weeks, or perhaps a month? You have all these good intentions, but life just seems to get in the way. You get hurried, distracted and the one thing you want to achieve becomes too hard to manage. Before long, you have pushed your plans to the back of the priority list to be handled later. Sound familiar?

What can you do to change this pattern you have set up for yourself? The first step is to find the trigger that makes you want to change habits. We all have triggers that makes us stop and be accountable to ourselves. That is when the real change can begin.

What is it you want to accomplish? Find what is deep within that will compel you to start down a path of change. Are you passionate about the process and the results it will give you?

There is a difference between thinking you want something and truly feeling a passion about what it will bring you. Think about how you feel when you have done something for the sole purpose of accomplishment or achievement. It comes from deep inside and you will push to reach the desired goal. The best part is the great feeling you have as you get closer to achieving your objective.

Think about times in your life you wanted to do something and had to work hard to achieve it. Now think about the feeling you had with each step of accomplishment. It was hard to do, but the reward is something you can't describe to another person. This feeling is personal and comes from a deep place within you. It is a connection to your inner self, and that is where the real self-work begins.

Here are a few things to think about as you start this journey of making desired change and reaching for what you have wanted and dreamed about:

First, slow down and then sit down. Take the time to think about what you want. Ask yourself these questions. Why do you want this? Think about the reasons and write them down. If you can't express them, you won't be able to act. What actions do you need to take to move forward with your desires? How long will it take you to accomplish this idea, goal or project? Is it a new habit you need to develop? Take notes and put thought into the details. Do you need support or an accountability plan? Will you have to overcome others who try to sabotage you with either words or actions? Write down a plan how to overcome these personal tests. Finally, decide how you will reward yourself for staying on track. Remember the desired change is the real reward but in the meantime what will give you the drive to keep pushing yourself?

Taking these steps can turn many of your dreams into reality. It takes planning and a commitment on your part. Most of all, you need to find the true reason why it is something you desire. Without knowing the **why,** you will not be inspired to do the **how** and **when**.

"Desire is the key to motivation, but it's determination and commitment to an unrelenting pursuit of your goal - a commitment to excellence - that will enable you to attain the success you seek." - Mario Andretti

RACING TO NOWHERE

One day I was driving to the office and came to a left turn at the stop light. The traffic was so heavy I could not get into the left turn lane which was empty. I needed about a half of car length to move forward and into the other lane. Because the space was too tight, I was stuck and had to wait. Suddenly a big truck came up behind me and jumped the curve and drove around me into the dirt and over to the turn lane. He raced down the empty lane to the intersection. About that same time, the traffic moved, and the next thing I know, I am sitting beside the truck at the stop light. At that moment, I realized the driver in the truck is a person racing to nowhere.

Do you find yourself in a rush and running to get to a destination? Humans in general are rushing for the next thing in life. As children we are excited about getting older. We are looking to the next birthday and proudly announce that we are almost to the next age. We cannot wait until we can legally drive, drink, vote, become an adult, have a holiday, or vacation. The list is endless.

This is a habit we begin at a young age and as we grow it grows.

The next thing we know we are impatient in traffic hurrying to get to the next designation.

But why do we hurry so much? One possibility to consider would be to look at our social environment. How many people do you know in a continual state of motion? They are juggling work, children schedules, on their phones while driving, cooking, or watching an event.

People take their work home to continue their projects and deadlines while watching television or during their evening meals. From all appearances, it looks like we believe juggling as much as possible makes us feel more productive.

There are expectations of what is to be accomplished. And we add to the pressure. We don't allow ourselves enough time to arrive at our destination. We put off projects until the last minute then race to get it done on time. After a while, we are in the habit of rushing and believe we don't have time for anything extra.

But if you will stop for a moment and take a deep breath, you will discover time is the same no matter how fast you go. You can control what you do with your time and enjoy life at a slower pace. There are so many things to enjoy during life, so don't rush and miss out.

Find your priorities and then learn to manage your time. This may mean saying no to invitations or other commitments you would have said yes to without a thought. It means you need to figure out what is important to you and plan to put that first.

You have the power to change your life and it starts by making small changes in your daily routine. Only you can stop your race to nowhere.

"There is more to life than increasing its speed." - Mohandas Gandhi

"Nature does not hurry, yet everything is accomplished." - Lao Tzu

LIFE GOES ON

There are moments in life we take for granted and then moments that bring us clarity. I have seen both. Within three years, I lost two sisters and my mother. With each passing, I was taught lessons I believe will be with me always.

Life doesn't wait for anything or anyone. It's fleeting and in constant motion. You can lose a loved one, experience failure or success, lose everything or win big, but life does not stop.

What we do from the moment of birth to the day we die is important. Living a worthwhile life is what I strive for as a goal. There is a poem called *The Dash*, by Linda Ellis. The poem is about the dash between the dates on the gravestone, the date born and the date of death. That dash represents an entire life and how that person lived. The poem reminds us that our material processions are not what are important but how we lived and loved and spent our time. Those moments of time are significant.

We have an opportunity to reach out to the world and do things that will make a difference in another's life. Lessons can be learned. Our experiences, knowledge, heartaches, hardships, loves, losses, successes and achievements can make us stronger. It's a choice taken every day. Choose to appreciate the people around you and live a life in accordance to your values and ideals.

We should savor all the joys, sorrows, happiness and sadness we experience every day. We should appreciate our life and all that happens around it because life goes on.

Be mindful of the present moment.

"In three words I can sum up everything I've learned about life: it goes on." - Robert Frost

ROLE MODELS

Some of us are fortunate enough to come across one special person. This is a person who gives to others in the form of teaching or mentoring. Many of us pursue mentoring in the workplace and other areas of our life. We have companies and clubs that have mentoring programs to get us up to speed and knowledgeable of the organization. These are worthy programs, but not what I am talking about here.

I am focusing on the teachers who will give their time and energy to help others learn and grow. These mentors do not look for recognition for their efforts nor do they announce their intentions. They use their knowledge to help others become better without looking for gratitude, only the satisfaction of guiding another.

Mentors do not set up rules and they do not reprimand, admonish, or make anyone uncomfortable. They lead by example with grace and dignity. Many times, the people they teach or help don't realize the effort until much later.

I was once so fortunate to have such a person in my life many years ago. This mentor was also the person I worked for at the time and, from the day I started with the company, she taught me about corporate structure, politics, internal and external relationships, as well as giving back to others and the community. Her spirit was open and friendly. She had patience and, instead of finding flaws, she saw opportunities. Although this was in a corporate environment, she taught me so much about life on a personal level. Her personal and work life was blurred when it came to her style and class. The same warm, friendly person who looked to get whatever was needed done was seen by all.

Sometimes, this very type of person is in our life to teach and mentor without us realizing the purpose. If you think you may value from learning from another but don't have a mentor in your life, take a few steps to learn from those around you. The first step is to make a commitment to search out people you would like to emulate their way of life. Think about what you are missing in your life and what you could improve upon.

If you are looking for a different lifestyle, search for people who appear to live the way you would like to live. Observe how they think and handle different situations in their life. How do they treat the people closest to them? What are their work ethics, spiritual path or community service? What are the qualities you find attractive that can be incorporated into your life? Do they have empathy? Are they honest, driven, fun or humorous?

By looking for these types of people, you will often find you need not have them guide you with scheduled meetings. By observing them, you will learn more about what your differences are and if you are willing to make and accept lifestyle changes.

Consider the possibility that you may be the person someone is looking to learn from and grow. If you can reach out to others with guidance or friendship, you could change a person's world. That is exactly what my dear friend and mentor did for me.

My friend passed away a few years ago. After our work together led us into different directions, we kept in touch with phone calls and an occasional lunch. She was always a shining example of the type of person I strive to be today. I can only hope I can provide and be that person to another.

"I think a role model is a mentor - someone you see on a daily basis, and you learn from them." - Denzel Washington

OVERWHELMED? THEN OVERCOME

Occasionally, I feel I have too much on my to-do list. Granted, I admit that many of those to-do list items are my own doing because I want to fit more into a day. Sometimes, I feel under the gun and have several projects needing to be completed at the same time. Now and then, I become inundated with so much I feel overwhelmed and so stressed that it becomes a problem.

Many years ago, I was working, going to college, had my sister with her three-year-old living with me, and was taking care of my home. It was just too much. With so many demands I ended up in a serious accident. I believe this happened because I was so overwhelmed and distracted.

My sister used to get overwhelmed from procrastination. It's an easy trap, and I have fallen into it as well. I put off things I find unpleasant or boring. It builds up and, before I know it, I am under a deadline to get that very thing done and the pressure begins.

At times we find ourselves at a dead-end. We don't know how to deal with what is causing us to have anxiety and feel weighed down. The results leave us feeling negative and berating ourselves. Here are a few tips to discover what core issue may be the cause and how to overcome being overwhelmed.

Are you procrastinating? If you see you are putting off the very thing that is causing your stress, try to develop a schedule or routine to deal with the problem. If you don't like to clean your home, try getting someone else to do it. Perhaps you have children to help and earn their allowance with chores or perhaps your budget will allow to hire help.

Look at your goals and see if you are adding too much to your plate at one time. You may be surprise what you can get done with a little planning and scheduling.

Planning and making a list will also show you need not juggle it all at once. Also by writing it down, you may find some of the things on your list are not necessary. If so delete it.

Look for and recognize the feelings you have when you are feeling overwhelmed. Take a moment to understand why you have those feelings and what you may do to change them.

Try to complete one project before you begin another. Frequently this is not possible, but if you organize and follow through, you will complete the task. You will feel accomplished and rewarded knowing it's done.

 Remember if you can discover what needs to be done, prioritize the tasks, break them down, and work on them one at a time, you will find you are moving forward and your projects will not seem to be such mountains.

"I know that each of us has much to do. Sometimes we feel

overwhelmed by the tasks we face. But if we keep our priorities in order, we can accomplish all that we should. We can endure to the end regardless of temptations, problems, and challenges." - Joseph B. Wirthlin

GETTING BACK FROM GIVING

I watched someone who had a major loss in his life and didn't miss a step giving back to his family. It's difficult juggling responsibilities, and this person works full-time and has a family of his own. Watching this person was a powerful learning experience for me.

In return, he gets back a grateful family who not only appreciates his efforts but is giving as much support as possible in return. The lesson here is to not focus on yourself, but to think about what you can do to help others. It will come back to you in a greater amount than the efforts you extended. Who would you rather work or deal with: someone who complains and blames or the one who takes responsibility and gets problems solved?

We alone control our environment, including our personal relationships, business challenges, and the social connections. Attitude is within our control. More and more today, I find people who want to avoid or evade any liability or burden they may have to endure. Responsibility has become a forgotten duty of everyday life. We don't want to be responsible for ourselves, children, or parents. We want someone else to take care of our lives by providing everything for us.

No one else can be responsible for you but you. There are no excuses. You are accountable by your actions and choices. Being accountable is following through with your commitments and responsibilities. The benefits for responsibility is worth the effort. It will develop your character, build your self-esteem, and develop trust with others.

"In the long run, we shape our lives, and we shape ourselves. The process never ends until we die. And the choices we make are ultimately our own responsibility." - Eleanor Roosevelt

GIVING AND GETTING

Have you ever wondered about people that seem to just be able to give without thought or purpose? They just do it. It's not a political, religious, or a charitable statement. It's something they do and believe it's the right thing with no regard for anything in return.

People are on a mission in life. It may be to make money, or to be the best in their field, or even perhaps just to survive the day. For many of us, our mission changes. Age plays a role in the change. We plan differently at several intervals of our life. What may have been a dream at twelve will be different at twenty, forty or seventy.

What mission are you on? As a business are you giving back to your customers and community? On a personal level, are you giving back to your family, friends, and organizations you believe in and want to support?

I believe individuals need take moments to reflect on the people they are thankful for and what they can do to help others. Think for an instant about the good feeling you get from helping others. It may be as little as helping a child discover something new, or perhaps doing something for a neighbor that needs a little extra help. That good feeling in your soul is the result of giving yourself. It's that something special you get in return.

Giving of yourself may also bring rewards of overall health. These rewards include longer life by generating better morale, boosting your immune system and a decrease in stress. Your overall outlook can improve and will motivate you to do more. Giving of yourself will also help you to better connect with others. You may see it draws more positive and like-minded people.

As you look forward to tomorrow, think how you can improve your life by giving to others, and don't be surprised at what comes back to you in return.

"If you want to lift yourself up, lift up someone else." - Booker T. Washington

MANAGING TRANSITION

Every day brings something new and different. Even if your life is a set schedule, or ingrained with habits, a multitude of circumstances can happen to make you happy, sad, shocked, or angry. I believe we forget how much we can change and achieve until we are forced to move. These changes in life or transitions have very distinct stages. The phases include an ending or letting go of a situation, a period of in-between which may be confusing or stressful and then a new beginning.

There are so many types of transitions in life. Many can be very difficult and others easy, but overall it is still change, nonetheless.

A few examples of transitions include changing jobs, moving to a new home, getting married, divorced or bringing a child into your life. Retiring, losing a loved one, or being on your own for the first time are also types of transitions that may be challenging.

These examples can transform or alter us into a different person depending on how we react.

This reminds me of a book, *Nothing is Impossible*, by Christopher Reeve. The book is a great example of transition and attitude. Reeve overcame incredible hardship when spinal cord injuries paralyzed him from the neck down. He went from being a film actor and director to becoming wheelchair-bound, requiring a respirator to breathe. His life-changing moment took him through the depth of despair to overcoming great odds. He became a spokesperson, writer, and created a paralysis foundation to promote research.

But outside of all those great accomplishments, he continued to be an involved husband, father, and friend until his death in 2004. He teaches us we have the choice to live with self-doubt and the fear of taking risks or to overcome and thrive. His story emphasizes the concept that life must be lived fully with gratitude and courage.

Having to manage change can be difficult, so here are a few things to consider while working through your transitions.

Take time to recognize you are going through a change and the need to allow yourself to work through it. Allow for closure. Keep an open mind and remember you may have several steps before feeling comfortable in your new setting, lifestyle, or environment.

Find a support system, along with education, and take care of youself. Embrace new beginnings and look to the future with the infinite possibilities available to you.

Are you making your transitions in life with purpose and resolution or are you looking backward hoping to keep life the same?

Your attitude is the difference that will overcome the difficult times and help when things don't go as planned.

Open your mind to accept each day and the path to your next step in life. With each step you grow in knowing yourself a little better and perhaps you will find your transitions in life will go smoother.

"Transitions in life can offer opportunities for discovery, provided we are open to random encounters and serendipitous events." - Robbie Shell

SETTING YOUR COMPASS

What you say and do provide the world with strong messages about your character and integrity. Are you sending the right messages? Are you leading people by your example? You alone have the power to change the way others view you.

Integrity is a little word that can be explained as a person who abides or is guided by a moral and ethical compass. Perhaps the best definition of integrity was defined by C. S. Lewis. He said it is, "Doing the right thing when no one is watching."

Another good example is the people who still function and do the right thing even when the world appears to be caving in around them. It's a trait that describes someone who has decent character, which does not wavier, and will be guided by what they know to be true and correct even if it's not convenient, easy, or best for them.

People of integrity show up and they show up on time, every time. They communicate well and are transparent with nothing to hide.

Another illustration of a person with integrity would be how they downplay their accomplishments and build up others. They do not have to be the center of attention because they are confident they are doing the right thing. Their self-esteem is secure within themselves. They know public opinion is not what matters and they don't have to bend their thoughts to please.

People of integrity lead because they fix problems rather than blame others. They don't lie or hide problems. They keep their word and don't have to make too many compromises because the people they lead feel secure and safe.

Here are a few places to begin if you are ready to work on building your integrity. Focus on yourself. Leave the gossip to others. Stay on your moral compass of being true to you. Be disciplined. Admit mistakes and use them to improve. Look for solutions. Keep your promises, and if you find you can't, then explain why immediately. Make a list of the top five things that you want to work on for yourself and review it daily.

One of the best ways to learn integrity is to find someone you believe lives by their moral compass and truly leads by example. Integrity plays an important role if you want to change people's thoughts and influence others.

"You are in integrity when the life you are living on the outside matches who you are on the inside." - Alan Cohen

FIND YOUR ROAD MAP

Do you often feel there is not enough time in the day? I ran a survey asking people how they felt about specific areas of life. The responses stood out like a flashing neon sign. "We want more time!"

Managing time becomes a juggling act. We look to find a balance between what we think needs done, what is important and to nurture our own mental and physical wellbeing. Some of the blocks of time we manipulate include work, children, spouse, aging parents, or people we allow to steal our time.

I have good news! There are choices you can make. The trick is to sort out what you want and where you want to be going forward. This road map can help you with direction so you can see what is important and the alternatives.

How do you begin? Start with taking a hard look at where you are now. Question where you want to be and if you are just letting life happen. Examine it closely and determine what is vital.

Make a commitment to yourself, but know every day you will have adjustments to your *"road map."* A good example is an airline flying from one city to another. There is a plan how to get there, but the course will have changes due to weather or other conditions. The pilot is still going to the destination, but decisions are altered to ensure arriving by the best and safest route. You can do the same. You may need modifications, but you still have a direction to keep you on your path.

Learn how to focus on what is important. Learn to compartmentalize your time so you can be more focused on the task at hand now. Be more cognitive of your time and check your *"road map"* often and see if you are on track.

"Just as your car runs more smoothly and requires less energy to go faster and farther when the wheels are in perfect alignment, you perform better when your thoughts, feelings, emotions, goals, and values are in balance." - Brian Tracy

CHECKS AND BALANCES

Each year many of us go through an annual medical check-up. I always find it reassuring when told I am in good health and shape for my age. But do we allow ourselves a personal evaluation of the other aspects in life such as career, finances, relationships, values, and growth?

I bring this up because we get so engrossed in our everyday activities, we forget to stop and look at the big picture of what we are doing.

I am talking about how our actions affect the lives of others. Periodically, you should stop and exam your life. Are you on the right path? Are you in control of your life or sliding by, letting the days melt into each other?

Here are a few areas I believe should be a focus to help bring more value to each day of life.

Do you know your talents and are you using them? You may have a hidden treasure. Finding these personal gems will allow you to grow. It may be as simple as sharing something you enjoy. Look for comments or compliments others have shared and see if it is something to cultivate.

Are you working towards better relationships? Relationships are paramount to achieving results and a better existence, whether you are looking at family or business. See where you can develop better and more meaningful associations and you may be surprise at the results.

Physical and mental health is a good place to start your checkup. Having good health leads to a good outlook and better attitude towards life. Take care of yourself.

Do you enjoy what you are doing for a living and, if not, why? It doesn't mean you must change positions or start over. Sometimes, it's as easy as an attitude change and looking at what you are doing in a new way. What can you do to lead the way to more success and happiness in your occupation?

Do you care for others? Leaders do, and they develop a culture of trust and accountability. Take a moment and look at the impressions you are sending out with your actions. You make an impression every day to those close as well as others watching from a distance.

Is it time to do a financial checkup? It may cause a change in spending habits. Look for patterns that need change to provide a more secure future.

Looking within is even more important. How we assess our spiritual life, community service, and values give more meaning and purpose to life. Discover more about these areas in yourself and you will cultivate more wisdom and deeper connections.

I cannot end these thoughts without saying what may be the most important point. To enjoy all that life offers, you need to have time to play. This brings more creativity and energy into your existence. Look for fun, laughter, and joy. Relish the little things that are offered to you each day. Embrace each new day with the thought of making it as special and full of meaning as possible.

"Live each day as if it were your last; love each day as if you will live forever." - Matshona Dhliwayo

FINDING THE JOY IN YOUR LIFE

A new year can begin any time you choose. You can do this by looking at your habits, goals, and dreams. Two questions I find good to ask when looking toward the future are: *Have I found joy and happiness in my life? Have I been able to share that with others?*

You may be familiar with the term *"bucket list."* I thought of it recently and how it's time to see if my list is still valid. I believe the list should represent the bucket list for life. Some of the things I had on my list have been checked off and others I have lost interest and deleted. New ideas and life changes have made me add to the list. So the list is a work in progress.

Do you have a list? It's a great way to think about what you would like to experience in life. By making notes, you are setting a course of where you will go.

The beginning of a new year is my time to look over what I wanted in the past and, rather than set New Year's resolutions, I work on my bucket list.

Your list can represent all aspects of your life. For example:

Work

You may want to change your career, develop better office relationships and become the best in your field. Perhaps you want to learn new skills that will help make your work easier or to stop habits that brings difficulty into your workplace.

Family and Friends

Spending more time or more quality time with your spouse, children or giving more attention to an elderly parent or friend may be your focus. Or perhaps helping a friend with a project or take their children for a day out may be on your list.

Health

Is it time for a mental and physical checkup? Perhaps you want to set aside quiet time to gather your thoughts and needs. Or you may want to focus on eating purposefully and moving your body more.

Contributions

It could be your time or money, but find something important to you. It may be taking part in an organization that makes you feel good or getting involved in an event that helps others. Give back.

Finances

Set goals, decide where you want to be, and make changes. Give up a latte or a fast food stop to put those dollars toward your next trip, car, or retirement. Shop smart. Be frugal.

Personal Development

Read, learn to play an instrument, dance, carve wood, write, train a dog, or appreciate the arts. Find a passion that makes you want to grow.

Play

Be young at heart. Jump on a park swing, parachute, plan a trip, start a game night. Look at what you have wanted to do, but have never taken time to put into motion.

Each person's bucket list will be unique. Some will have only a few items while others will have many. Remember your life will change and so shall the list. Don't look at it as work when creating your list. Remember this is a wish list of things you want to experience in life.

DARE TO DREAM

Every day, someone has a dream that has the potential to take them to a new place in life. Dreams come in all sizes. Some are big, some small, but all are very important.

Think where our world would be without the pursuit of individual dreams. Our dreams have led the world to new and exciting advancements. Dreams of exploration have led us from the deepest parts of the ocean to the farthest places in the galaxy. Specific dreams have changed the way we view our world, how we travel, care for our health, and develop as nations.

We hold so much power with our dreams! The world is truly directed from our imagination and vision. Isn't it fascinating and exciting?

Why don't we use our dreams more to help us with our goals, passion and daily living? People that are true visionaries have a drive to continue working toward a purpose in life. And while they are working on those dreams, they are finding fulfilment. Passion can fire up a dream and propel it to a life of its own.

You may have dreams sitting on a shelf and have not acted upon them. Some of you may fear you will fail, while others are thinking their friends will laugh at their ideas. Another group just doesn't have enough faith to act upon their visions. Also, a handful don't want to proceed on their ideas because they lack support, financially or otherwise.

Here are guidelines to think about when you are ready to act upon your dream.

Is your goal realistic? Are you thinking about the results and not the journey? Have you put thought into the details? And what do you expect will happen when you achieve your dream? It could change your world.

Don't let these questions derail your intentions. Many dreams are simple, while others are complicated. If your dream is giving back to the community, then it may be as easy as volunteering at the local non-profit of your choice. On the flip side, if you are looking to manufacture a product, you will have homework to prepare.

Whatever your dream; act, believe in yourself and expect some bumps and turns along the way. It is possible to make your dreams a reality, but it takes effort to plan, be consistent, and overcome the obstacles. Remember dreams are the essence of creativity and we have the power to decide how we use them.

"If you can dream it, you can do it." - Walt Disney

"I say to you today, my friends, that in spite of the difficulties and frustrations of the moment, I still have a dream." - Martin Luther King, Jr.

RANDOM THOUGHTS

ABOUT THE AUTHOR

Robin Anne Griffiths has spent a lifetime working with a variety of personalities and business organizations focusing on building lasting relationships. As a certified master coach and personal trainer, Griffiths works with people on a journey for change and her work includes helping women though life changing transitions and to create personal balance –
physically and mentally.

Robin Anne Griffiths lives in Southwest Florida with her husband, rescue dogs and eclectus parrot.

www.robinannegriffiths.com